GOD'S

Mission

GOD'S

Song

JOYCE D. SOHL

HYMN EDITORS:
S T KIMBROUGH, JR.
CARLTON R. YOUNG

Women's Division • General Board of Global Ministries • The United Methodist Church

ISBN 1-890569-96-8
Library of Congress Control Number 2006933706

Printed in the United States of America.

CONTENTS

T he history of mission and missionary activity of the church has been studied and researched by many authors, historians, and theologians. As United Methodist Women, many of us can recite the important dates within the history of our organization starting with the formation of the Woman's Foreign Missionary Society, Methodist Episcopal Church in 1869. Few though have studied music and hymnody as an important part of missionary endeavors. This study is a beginning step in exploring the relationship between mission and hymnody.

Robert A. Schneider, in his recent paper about hymns and foreign mission, says:

> Hymns were intertwined with every aspect of the missionary enterprise. Participants in the movement wrote, published, read, meditated upon, and sang hymns to express their core beliefs, to give voice to their visions of the future, and to strengthen their individual and collective commitment to the cause. They used hymns to communicate their beliefs, visions, and commitment to other Christians, to their society, and to prospective new Christians around the world.[1]

Hymns were used by missionaries to proclaim the gospel to new converts. Hymns were sung at missionary society meetings to motivate giving and prayers for the mission endeavors. Hymns were used to call persons to become missionaries or deaconesses. Hymns described mission fields and repeated Christ's command "to make disciples." Hymns sustained many missionaries and deaconesses as they "labored in the vineyard."

Hopefully, the chapters in this text can help us gain an understanding of the role of music and hymns in mission. Biblical understandings of mission and hymns that reflect the scriptural references are explored in Chapter 1. John Wesley's teachings on mission are looked at briefly along with several of Charles Wesley's mission hymns. In addition, a variety of definitions of mission are given.

Selected early missionary hymns are discussed in Chapter 2 as well as changes in the theology of mission reflected in the hymns and mission activities. Chapter 3 looks at the holiness movement and its impact on social reform and the social gospel movement and its understanding of mission.

The missionaries and their music are the emphases of Chapter 4. Included are a brief discussion of ethnomusicology, some stories about the use of hymns in mission, and learnings from a survey of active and retired missionaries and deaconesses. In Chapter 5, hymns about current justice issues are discussed including hymns about peace, the environment, poverty, and children.

The movement during the last part of the twentieth century toward global song is the focus of Chapter 6. Included are a look at the Global Praise Program of the General Board of Global Ministries of The United Methodist Church and interviews with contemporary musicians about new mission hymnody and the need to sing each other's song. Hymns with words and music are included for easy reference and use.

A bibliography, an index of persons mentioned within the text, and an index of hymns quoted or cited within the text are also included. The study guide is at the end of this book.

In the writing of this book several different research methods were used. Interviews were conducted with selected hymn writers, musicians, and missionaries. Diaries, books, and papers of some missionaries and musicians were reviewed. Selected journals, minutes, and publications of mission organizations, especially within the United Methodist tradition, were also reviewed. A variety of hymnals from the predecessor churches of The United Methodist Church and other denominations, Sunday school and evangelistic music, and contemporary global music were used as the source of hymns. The hymns used in this text are illustrative of the large number of "missionary hymns" available. Of course all hymns have not been included and the selection was done by me based on the needs of the study.

Carlton Young has described mission hymns as "an unique body of hymnody that blends the message of missions with the work of mission: raising money, recruitment of missionaries, and description of people and lands."[2] As we pursue this "unique body of hymnody" may we remember that the call to involvement in God's mission comes to each of us, even as we sing God's songs.

Special thanks are extended to all musicians, writers, missionaries, and deaconesses who were willing to be interviewed or responded to a questionnaire. Thanks are also given to Carlton R. Young and S T Kimbrough, Jr. for their helpful knowledge and expertise regarding hymnody; and to readers Toby Gould, Lois Dauway, and members and staff of the Spiritual and Theological Concerns Committee of the Women's Division.

God's mission is enabled by God's songs. God's songs are inspired by God's mission. Sing God's songs as you participate in God's mission.

Joyce D. Sohl

[1] Robert A. Schneider, "Jesus Shall Reign: Hymns and Foreign Missions, 1800-1870," *Wonderful Words of Life* (Grand Rapids, Mich.: William B. Eerdmans Publishing Company, 2004), 77.

[2] Carlton R. Young, "Christian Global Song: Missional and Musical Perspectives," (Unpublished Hugh T. McElrath Lectures, The Southern Baptist Theological Seminary, October 2001), 3.

CHAPTER 1

"To tell to all the world that God is light."

— Mary A. Thomson

I n the midst of singing "O Zion, Haste" in church on Sunday, Marjorie started to think to herself: "What am I really singing? Do I believe what I am singing? What is this hymn all about? Who is Mary A. Thomson?" On the way home Marjorie couldn't get the tune out of her head and her questions returned. She knew some serious research, prayer, and conversation were needed to answer at least some of her questions. She also thought that Pastor Janice might be helpful. A few weeks later Marjorie wrote the following information in her computer-journal:

"O Zion, Haste" (#66) was written by Mary A. Thomson in 1868. Born in London in 1834, she later came to Philadelphia. Her husband was a librarian and the couple had several children. She wrote about 40 hymns, some of them published in the hymnal of the Episcopal Church in 1892, and she died in 1923. Mary Thomson wrote "O Zion, Haste" while she was nursing one of her children with typhoid fever, and used the tune by James Walch that she knew. This hymn was published in 1894 and first appeared in *The Methodist Hymnal* of 1905. In that hymnal there were two more stanzas that do not appear in *The United Methodist Hymnal* of 1989.

> 'Tis thine to save from peril of perdition
>   The souls for whom the Lord his life laid down;
> Beware lest, slothful to fulfill thy mission,
>   Thou lose one jewel that should deck his crown.
>
> He comes again; O Zion, ere thou meet him,
>   Make known to every heart his saving grace;
> Let none whom he hath ransomed fail to greet him,
>   Through thy neglect, unfit to see his face.[1]

As a teacher of English literature in the local community college, Marjorie knew how to do research. She enjoyed digging into a topic. She also was what she called an "unprofessional" piano player, playing the piano in the evening to relax while her two teenagers were doing homework to their own music.

Now Marjorie was ready to have a conversation with Pastor Janice about the meaning of the hymn. She made an appointment and asked her friend Louise to join her. Louise had recently retired after years of teaching music in the local high school and directing several church choirs. Marjorie felt the combination of Louise with her professional expertise and Pastor Janice with her extensive library and interest in the mission of the church would be very helpful.

They had a wonderful time exploring the hymn. Pastor Janice added to the conversation by mentioning some material she had recently found and both Marjorie and Louise felt they were spiritually enriched through the sharing. Later Marjorie put in writing a summary of their conversation, centering on the scriptural basis of the hymn and some of its themes. She sent it to Louise and Pastor Janice via email.

The scriptural basis for this hymn probably came from several sources. Perhaps Mary Ann Thomson had in mind Isaiah 40:9-11. Here, at the beginning of what is known as Second Isaiah, the poetry speaks of "good tidings" using the Hebrew word *basar*, which became the word used for "gospel" in later Scriptures. Isaiah was helping the dejected Israelites realize that God was in their midst providing good news for the people. He proclaimed that God was willing to intervene in their history. Later God intervened again with the coming of Jesus and the message of the new reign of God.[2]

It is also possible that Thomson had in mind the Great Commission found in Matthew 28:18-20. She writes of proclaiming the glad tidings to "every people, tongue, and nation" which could well be her way of stating "make disciples of all nations." She also could, in her references to light and darkness, be referring to Jesus as the Light of the World or to the many places where Jesus admonishes his followers to walk in the light (see Matthew 4:16, Luke 2:32, John 3:21, John 8:12).

Proclamation of the salvation of Jesus is an obvious theme of the hymn and the responsibility of all who sing the hymn. Thomson believes that all are eligible for salvation and that God does not want "one soul to perish." There is concern expressed about the many who are without the knowledge of Jesus or who are "bound in the darksome prison house of sin." At the same time she realizes that there are many people "with none to tell them" of salvation through Jesus the Christ.

In the third stanza God is seen as love and present in the lives of every person in the world, whether they accept God or not. In other words God initiates salvation. This is a profound phrase, putting the role of God and the role of the missionary in perspective.

The last stanza speaks directly to women of the last quarter of the nineteenth century. Most church women of that time were homemakers and active in their missionary organizations.[3] Most likely they could not go as a missionary but they could:

1. "give of thine own to bear the message glorious" meaning to send their sons and daughters to be missionaries;
2. "give of thy wealth to speed them on their way" meaning to give of their financial resources;
3. "pour out thy soul for them in prayer victorious" meaning to pray for those who proclaimed the gospel and those who heard the "glad tidings."[4]

"O Zion, Haste" is a hymn written by a homemaker with a strong sense of commitment to Jesus, with an understanding of God's presence in the life of every person, and with knowledge that every follower of Christ can and should participate in God's mission.

Marjorie and Louise were now eager to look at other mission hymns. They decided to start by seeing what the Bible said about mission and how hymn writers have used the Scriptures in their hymns. Then perhaps they would see what John and Charles Wesley said and wrote about mission. They knew they were at the beginning of a long, but exciting, journey.

Biblical Understandings of Mission

Many of us, when asked to give a biblical text regarding mission, immediately go to the so-called Great Commission in the last chapter of Matthew. We fail to realize that there are other equally valid biblical texts that challenge the followers of Christ to be in mission. A variety of biblical texts have been the basis of mission hymns. Sometimes the connection between the biblical text and the hymn is obvious; at other times it is a compilation of biblical writings that comes together in the poetry of the hymn.

Micah 6:8

Micah 6:8 has been the source of several hymns. Some writers have simply taken the text and set it to music. Others, like Albert F. Bayly (1901–1984), used the text as the basis for a hymn. "What Does the Lord Require" (#47) looks very closely at the actions of rulers, the wealthy, and corporations. Stanza two is addressed to the "rulers of earth" and questioned their understanding of justice in the midst of increased crime and cruelty. In stanza three those that "gain wealth by trade" are admonished to care for their workers and not be greedy. In stanza four, Bayly states that God's law is difficult and can only be fulfilled through the grace of Christ allowing us to do justice, love mercy, and walk humbly with God. Albert F. Bayly was a Congregational minister in England.

Matthew 28:18-20

Most modern scholars are clear that the Matthew Commission (Matthew 28:18-20) must be taken against the background of the entire Matthew Gospel. Leon Adkins (1896–1986) was a Methodist pastor and worked for the Board of Education of the Methodist Church from 1955 to 1966.[5] In his hymn, "Go, Make of All Disciples" (#10), Adkins emphasizes God's role in the "making of disciples." The phrases "let our daily living reveal thee everywhere" and "each life's vocation accents thy holy way" indicate that discipleship is as costly for those who witness as for those who receive the good news. The actions and teachings of Jesus as found in Matthew become the model for discipleship. This would include the Beatitudes in Matthew 5; the parables of the kingdom (Matthew 13); and the Great Commandment (Matthew 22:37-40). In stanza one, learning is to be inspired "through earnest, fervent prayer" for both the witness and the new disciple. Stanza four acknowledges the enormity of the task, the guidance of the Spirit, and the goal of the reign of God.

Luke 24:49, Acts 1:8, and Luke 4:16-21

Luke, in writing both the Gospel of Luke and Acts, emphasized the role of the Holy Spirit as the followers of Jesus witnessed to the Resurrection (see Luke 24:49 and Acts 1:8). It was the Holy Spirit that would give power to the believer. It was the Holy Spirit that would make the witnesses bold in telling about Jesus. The Holy Spirit came at Pentecost as was promised by Jesus and from then on the men and women of the early church witnessed to God's mighty acts in the world. They were persecuted, imprisoned, faced disagreements among themselves, and were sometimes afraid, but they followed the catalyst of the Holy Spirit.

Brian Wren (b. 1936) in "There's a Spirit in the Air" (#43), expands the Pentecost story to include the passage from the prophet Isaiah that Jesus read in the temple at the beginning of his ministry (see Luke 4:16-21). Wren writes of God working through the Spirit in the world today, of feeding the hungry, of caring for the stranger and the homeless, and of turning wrong into right. The hymn has a personal Pentecost message "to lose your shyness" and tell of God's deeds. But there is also a message for the community of believers to share in communion, do acts of mercy, and reveal the love of Jesus. The last stanza becomes a prayer that the Spirit may "fill our praise, guide our thoughts and change our ways." This is followed by the final affirmation that "God in Christ has come to stay" and Christians are to live the reign of God here and now. Brian Wren is a teacher, ordained minister in the British Congregational Church, and a writer of hymns. He is now living in the United States. He encourages congregations to sing this hymn with "joyful, energetic praise" and let it become "a joyful dance."[6]

John 20:19-23

Fred Pratt Green (1903–2000), in "The Church of Christ, in Every Age" (#41), writes of the church as an instrument of God's mission. In the hymn he identifies the responsibilities of the church as: 1) to be Spirit led, 2) to act to eliminate injustice in the world, and 3) to be the "servant church" and "a partner in Christ's sacrifice." Green was a minister in the British Methodist Church and one of the great hymn writers of the twentieth century. He believed that "the gospel has social implications too often overlooked in a materialistic society."[7]

The scriptural basis of this hymn could be from several sources. One of those is John 20:19-23. The disciples are behind closed doors. They are frightened for they do not understand Mary's story of seeing Jesus. Then Jesus appears to them, gives them the Holy Spirit, and sends them out into the world. Jesus' statement: "As the Father has sent me, so I send you" is the beginning of mission as exhibited by the life and teaching of Jesus. Green picks this up in stanzas three and four with his strong statements on the servant role of the church. He also emphasizes that it is Christ who teaches his followers to care for the world. The last stanza defines mission as being in obedience to Christ to care for the world and to spread the Word.

Ephesians 4:1-16

Paul is often viewed as the first missionary. His strategy of proclaiming the gospel in strategic cities and to a variety of people brought many converts. In the letters he wrote to the churches in Corinth, Ephesus, Galatia, and elsewhere he articulates a complex understanding of mission. His theology of mission includes a strong belief of unity in the midst of diversity, an active preaching of salvation through Jesus Christ, the inclusiveness of the gospel, and living a life that attracts persons to Jesus.

Rusty Edwards (b. 1955), a Lutheran pastor in Illinois, has written "We All Are One in Mission" (#3) that picks up some of Paul's under-standing of mission as found in Ephesians 4:1-16. In the first and third stanzas, emphasis is put on oneness in call and mission, a variety of gifts that unites, and a single plan for working together "that all may know Christ's love." In the second stanza the concept of service, witness, and ministry are tied together through a common purpose and God's grace. The goal of mission is seen to be unity in Christ brought about by the Word of God.

John and Charles Wesley

In 1735, just three weeks after the death of their father, John and Charles Wesley sailed for Georgia. They arrived in early February 1736 after having survived a difficult journey. Also on their ship was a group of Moravians with a strong but simple faith in the continuing presence of God in their lives. The Moravians were on their way as missionaries to the Native Americans in Georgia. These German pietists taught the Wesleys their hymns. John later translated thirty-three Moravian hymns into English. The Wesleys worked some with the Native Americans while in Georgia, but primarily ministered to the colonists. Their "missionary journey" was less than two years in duration.

Among the hymns that John Wesley (1703–1791) translated are several stanzas from a hymn by Johann Joseph Winckler (1670–1722).

> Shall I, for fear of feeble man,
> Thy Spirit's course in me restrain?
> Or, undismay'd, in deed and word
> Be a true witness for my Lord?
>
> The love of Christ doth me constrain
> To seek the wand'ring souls of men;
> With cries, entreaties, tears, to save,
> To snatch them from the gaping grave.[8]

Here Winckler is raising questions about the tension between the urging of the Spirit and people's opinion about how a Christian should witness to the Christ. This question is one all Christians can ask regarding their own participation in God's mission. The hymn declares that the love of Christ motivates one to seek out the lost.

John Wesley believed in and practiced what he called "Works of Mercy," a central understanding of mission to United Methodists. He described these as:

> The feeding the hungry, the clothing the naked, the enter-taining or assisting the stranger, the visiting those that are

sick or in prison, the comforting the afflicted, the instructing the ignorant, the reproving the wicked, the exhorting and encouraging the well-doer; and if there be any other work of mercy, it is equally included in this direction. (Sermon, "Upon our Lord's Sermon on the Mount, VI," 1748)

Not only did John Wesley preach about mission, but Charles Wesley (1707–1788) wrote mission hymns which Methodists were encouraged to sing and pray. "Lord of the Harvest, Hear" is based on Luke 10:1-20. It is the story of the seventy sent out by Jesus and their experiences and feelings. This could well be the first story of lay missionary service. The poem is addressed to God seen as the "Lord of the harvest." It is a prayer with petitions regarding the needs of the faithful, a need for more workers, and spreading the "gospel word." Workers are called by God to preach the gospel, proclaim God's grace, and call all persons unto Christ.

> Lord of the harvest, hear
> Thy needy servants cry;
> Answer our faith's effectual prayer,
> And all our wants supply.
>
> On thee we humbly wait,
> Our wants are in thy view;
> The harvest truly, Lord, is great,
> The laborers are few.
>
> Convert, and send forth more
> Into thy Church abroad;
> And let them speak thy word of power,
> As workers with their God.
>
> Give the pure gospel word,
> The word of general grace;
> Thee let them preach, the common Lord,
> Savior of human race.
>
> Oh, let them spread thy name,
> Their mission fully prove,
> Thy universal grace proclaim,
> Thy all-redeeming love.

> On all mankind forgive
> > Empower them still to call,
> And tell each creature under heaven
> > That thou hast died for all.[9]

The hymn, "Your Duty Let the Apostle Show" (#73), is based on Acts 20:35. Within this hymn Charles Wesley cites the "Works of Mercy" that his brother John preached. In stanza two is a listing of some of these "works" and the indication that giving is blessed. The true disciple is to labor for Jesus, use one's hands for God, and do all because of love. In the last stanza reference is made to Matthew 25:31-46 where Jesus reminds his followers that when they help their neighbor they are ministering unto Jesus.

The story of the women who went to the tomb on the resurrection morning is told in "Hallelujah, Christ is Risen" (#52). The story is recorded in Luke 24 as well as in more detail in John 20. In the hymn the women are called courageous, grace-filled, proclaimers of the resurrection power, and powerful witnesses. These women told the "joyful tidings," they taught the apostles about the Resurrection, and they received life and pardon through the resurrection of Jesus. The last stanza is a prayer that the singer might hear their message and "wonder and believe." Note the similarities between this hymn and the chorus of "O Zion, Haste."

Mission is....

There are several mission themes that can be ascertained from the hymns and Scriptures explored above. They include justice, salvation, proclamation of the gospel, love, a calling to service, inclusiveness, etc. Themes are easy to identify, but how is mission defined? Here are a few definitions from contemporary theologians:

> Mission is the participation of Christians in the liberating mission of Jesus, wagering on a future that verifiable experience seems to belie. It is the good news of God's love, incarnated in the witness of a community, for the sake of the world.[10]
> > — David J. Bosch

Mission is not a burden laid upon the church; it is a gift and a promise to the church that is faithful.[11]

— Lesslie Newbigin

Mission is participation in healing in all aspects of life: spiritual, physical, sociocultural, and political.[12]

— Omega Bula

Mission is witnessing to Jesus, a confessing of Jesus and the God who sent him, and an abiding in him.[13]

— Teresa Okure

Mission is participating and communicating in God's ceaseless energy of cosmic healing and whole-making....Mission is the communication of love in action.[14]

— Mary Grey

Mission is the action of the God of grace who creates out of love, who calls a covenant community, who graciously redeems and reconciles a broken and sinful people in Jesus Christ, and who through the Holy Spirit calls the church into being as the instrument of the good news of grace to all people. Mission is also the church's grateful response to what God has done, is doing, and will do.[15]

— Mission Statement of
The United Methodist Church

Mission is witnessing to the rule of God through words and deeds...It is an on-going activity of the living God who transforms, heals, and reconciles.[16]

— Glory E. Dharmaraj

Songwriters have also given various definitions of mission. In "Sois la Semilla" ("You Are the Seed") (#31) by Cesáreo Gabaraín (1936–1991), a parish priest and Spanish musician, metaphors are used to describe mission activities. Some of the metaphors are those used by Jesus in his stories about the reign of God. All describe what it means to be people participating in God's mission. In the first stanza God's friends are the seed, a star, the yeast, a small grain of salt, a beacon, the dawn, the wheat, a sting, and a gentle touch as they witness. The list goes on in stanzas two and three to include the flame, shepherds, friends, the new kingdom, life, waves in a turbulent sea, and a new loaf of bread. The chorus calls "my friends" to proclaim, to forgive, and to witness to the resurrection of Christ. The new kingdom is defined as one of justice and truth. The good deeds are always to show a way to God. This is a powerful hymn that expands upon the Great Commission in Matthew 28 and the stories of the kingdom in Matthew 13. It provides images that can cause numerous discussions on the meaning of mission and the responsibility to participate in God's mission.

Marjorie and Louise persuaded Pastor Janice to use this hymn as a basis for a special study on mission as seen in the Gospel of Matthew. They thought the images in the hymn would make a great Bible study.

[1] *The Methodist Hymnal* (New York: Eaton & Mains and Cincinnati: Jennings & Graham, 1905), 654.

[2] Walter Brueggemann, *An Introduction to the Old Testament* (Louisville, Ky.: Westminster John Knox Press, 2003), 168.

[3] Remember that the Woman's Foreign Missionary Society was organized in 1869.

[4] June Hadden Hobbs, *"I Sing for I Cannot Be Silent"* (Pittsburgh: University of Pittsburgh Press, 1997), 131-132.

[5] Carlton R. Young, *Companion to The United Methodist Hymnal* (Nashville: Abingdon Press, 1993), 714.

[6] Brian Wren, *Praying Twice* (Louisville, Ky.: Westminster John Knox Press, 2000), 79.

[7] Paul Westermeyer, *With Tongues of Fire* (St. Louis, Mo.: Concordia Publishing House, 1995), 89.

[8] *Wesley Hymn Book* (London: A. Weekes & Co, 1960), #124.

[9] Frank Whaling, editor, *John and Charles Wesley* (Mahwah, N. J.: Paulist Press, 1981), 289-290.

[10] David J. Bosch, *Transforming Mission* (Maryknoll, N.Y.: Orbis Books, 1991), 519.

[11] Lesslie Newbigin, *Mission in Christ's Way* (New York: Friendship Press, 1987), 40.

[12] Omega Bula, "Women in Mission Participating in Healing," *International Review of Mission* Vol. LXXXI No. 322 (April 1992): 247.

[13] Teresa Okure, "The Significance Today of Jesus' Commission to Mary Magdalene," *International Review of Mission* Vol. LXXXI No. 322 (April 1992): 178.

[14] Mary Grey, "She is a Great Man!" *International Review of Mission* Vol. LXXXI No. 322 (April 1992): 203, 210.

[15] "Grace Upon Grace," The Mission Statement of The United Methodist Church (Nashville: Graded Press, 1990), 4.

[16] Glory E. Dharmaraj, *Concepts of Mission* (New York: The Women's Division, 1999), 9, 23.

CHAPTER 2

"Peoples and realms of every tongue dwell on his love with sweetest song."

— Isaac Watts

One cold winter evening Marjorie got a call from Louise. She was all excited about a box of old hymnals she had found in her attic. Some of them were "a little strange," but most were from Methodist or Evangelical United Brethren traditions. She felt they now had a gold mine from which to gather more information about mission hymns. Louise wanted to do some initial work on the hymnals. She also felt a meeting in a couple of weeks to review what she had found would be helpful.

Louise ended up spending a good deal of time with the hymnals. Her enthusiasm increased as she found other hymnals in the church library and a few books that told about the writers and musicians. She also discovered a book that gave a brief history of the missionary movement. She eventually wrote a summary paper, organizing her findings and putting things in perspective. This she sent as an email attachment to Marjorie and Pastor Janice prior to their meeting.

Early Missionary Societies and Missionary Hymns

Missionary societies developed in England and the United States during the last part of the eighteenth century and the first quarter of the nineteenth century. In 1792 the Baptist Missionary Society was formed in England and a year later William Carey was sent as a missionary to India. He had been instrumental in convincing his fellow pastors that conversion of the heathen was the responsibility of the current followers of Jesus. From his sermon at the formation meeting of the society came the missionary motto, "Expect great things from God: attempt great things for God."

The theme hymn for the early missionary societies was "Jesus Shall Reign" (#18) by Isaac Watts (1674–1748). Watts was a well-educated man, fluent in English, Greek, Latin, and Hebrew. He was for a short time a pastor in an Independent Chapel in London, but for most of his life he was a family tutor and chaplain and a writer of theological and philosophical books and hymns. Watts strongly believed in congregational singing. He advocated that hymns should be in words that the people understood and that the Psalms should be Christianized. He thus wrote and published hymns that fulfilled his two primary concerns. His hymns were sung by the people of the Dissenting churches because of their simplicity, biblical content, and ease of singing to familiar tunes.

In 1719 Watts published *The Psalms of David Imitated in the Language of the New Testament, and Apply'd to the Christian State and Worship.* "These lyrics were not metrical translations, nor even paraphrases; they were inspired by Psalms and they followed in general the thoughts of the original, but they contained a great deal of Watts."[1] "Jesus Shall Reign" was inspired by Psalm 72 and became the first great missionary hymn seventy-five years later. Watts changed the psalm from a prayer of support for King Solomon into a song of praise to Jesus as ruler of the world. New Testament passages that might have influenced the hymn are Matthew 28:19-20; Luke 4:16-20; Mark 10:3-16; and Revelation 21:3-4.

Both Carey's motto and Watts's hymn reached the United States and were received with enthusiasm. People were sending money to England for Carey's work and preachers were soon considering the merits of forming a similar society in the United States. By 1810 the American Board of Commissioners for Foreign Missions was started by a group of primarily Congregational ministers in Massachusetts. Two years later that society sent out Adoniram and Ann Judson to India as missionaries. It is significant that Ann Judson was also commissioned as a missionary, the first of many married and single women to answer God's call.

The missionary movements developed out of revivals which were fueled by:

> * theological discussions on eschatology brought about by the turn of the century;

* exploration of the world by James Cook and others implying that God was opening up the world to mission; and
* an intense concern about sharing the love and salvation of Christ with all.[2]

As the missionary movement increased in Europe and the United States hymns were written to tell the story of missions, proclaim the theology of mission, inspire giving to missions, and challenge people to accept the call to missionary service. Such hymns were sung in the local church, at missionary agency meetings, and at women's missionary meetings. In hymnals these hymns appeared under the title "Missionary Hymns" or "Missions." They included hymns for both children and adults.

Several of Mrs. Vokes's missionary hymns were published in 1797 in *A Selection of Missionary and Devotional Hymns*. Nothing is known about Mrs. Vokes except that she lived in England.[3] "Behold, The Heathen Waits to Know" is one of her hymns. Thoughts expressed in the hymn include:

* the heathen are those who do not know Jesus;
* thanksgiving should be given for the opportunity to labor, give, and pray for missions;
* praise is given for proclaiming the gospel; and
* God's grace is available to all.

The last stanza is very inclusive and probably refers to I Corinthians 12:13. This stanza looks expectantly toward the time when "sweet incense to his Name shall rise" throughout the world. Vokes obviously sees that much work needs to be done.

> Behold, the heathen waits to know
> The joy the Gospel will bestow;
> The exiled captive to receive
> The freedom Jesus has to give.
>
> Come, let us, with a grateful heart,
> In this blest labour share a part;
> Our prayers and off'rings gladly bring
> To aid the triumphs of our King.

Our hearts exult in songs of praise,
That we have seen these latter days,
When our Redeemer shall be known,
Where Satan long hath held his throne.

Where'er his hand hath spread the skies,
Sweet incense to his Name shall rise;
And slave and freeman, Greek and Jew,
By sov'reign grace be form'd anew.[4]

Thomas Gibbons (1720–1785) was a clergyman of the Independent Church in England. "Great God! The Nations of the Earth" acknowledges that every nation of the earth is God's and the gospel is sent to all. In the third stanza Gibbons raises the question "when shall these glad tidings spread the spacious earth around?" The fourth stanza is a prayer for God to bless each attempt at spreading the gospel and destroying sin.

Great God! The nations of the earth
    Are by creation thine;
And in thy works, by all beheld,
    Thy power and glory shine.

But, Lord, thy greater love hath sent
    Thy gospel to mankind,
Unveiling what rich stores of grace
    Are treasured in thy mind.

Oh, when shall these glad tidings spread
    The spacious earth around,
Till every tribe and every soul
    Shall hear the joyful sound?

Smile, Lord, on each divine attempt
    To spread the gospel's rays,
And build on sin's demolished throne
    The temples of thy praise.[5]

There were key words that appeared in many of the missionary hymns. "Zion" has several meanings in the Bible: a citadel; a sacred mountain; a metaphor for security; the Temple area in Jerusalem; the city of David; metaphor for the church.[6] In hymns "Zion" is used as a metaphor for the church, the new city of God, or the people called to proclaim the gospel to the world. Refer again to "O Zion, Haste" (#66) as an illustration of this meaning.

"Light" and "darkness" were used to describe the difference between those who had accepted Jesus and those who had not heard of him. Nations were often described as dark, meaning pagan or Satan-filled. Light came from Jesus; light was part of God's creation; light was like the morning sun. In the first stanza of "Though Now the Nations Sit Beneath" darkness describes the nations that are covered by death due to their lack of knowledge of Jesus. It is God's light that will make the "holy towers to shine."

> Though now the nations sit beneath
> The darkness of o'erspreading death,
> God will arise with light divine,
> On Zion's holy towers to shine.[7]

This hymn was written by Leonard Bacon (1802–1881), a Congregational minister in New Haven, Connecticut. He was the son of a missionary to the Native Americans in Michigan and had an intense missionary zeal. This led him to establish a monthly "Missionary Concert" for the promotion of missions and the recruitment of missionaries.[8] The missionary hymns were sung at these meetings and soon such concerts were appearing throughout New England. New hymns were often introduced and prayers were raised for the work of missions.

Cecil Frances Alexander (1818 or 1823–1895), in her hymn "Souls in Heathen Darkness Lying" (#77), suggests the urgency that many felt for the conversion of the heathen. This urgency was not only for the unconverted but also for the messenger. Christians were responsible for spreading the gospel and since "Jesus' sacrifice had bought all heathen souls, it was the duty of the first-saved to teach all other nations."[9] Alexander implies this duty in the third stanza by making essential the spreading of the gospel for a good report at the final judgment. Throughout this hymn darkness and light are used as metaphors for salvation or its lack. She calls on the Spirit to "go before" the missionary to seek those who have not seen God's light.

Shifts in Mission Theology

A different theology of mission appeared in many of the hymns written following the beginning of the nineteenth century. The hymns reflected changes in mission theology taking place in missionary societies. David Bosch writes that in the missionary movement "a not-so subtle shift had occurred in the original love motive; compassion and solidarity had been replaced by pity and condescension."[10] Not only were the heathen seen as living in darkness, but entire countries and continents were described as dark. Bosch goes on to say that "love had deteriorated into patronizing charity" and a sense of spiritual superiority developed among the missionaries and their supporters.[11] In some hymns not only was spiritual superiority declared, but one's country was seen to be superior.

Julia Haskell Sampson wrote "Over the Ocean Wave." Nothing is known about the writer. In the first stanza heathen are described as poor, ignorant, far away, and waiting for the gospel. The chorus calls for pity and encourages haste in spreading the gospel. The last words of the chorus though, imply that those without Christ are requesting the missionary "to come." In the second stanza light is used to describe the land of the sender because of "God's own word." Bibles, teachers, preachers, and more are needed and must be sent. The last stanza describes "the heathen band" as receiving the missionaries with joy and thankfulness for "guiding us home." This hymn is addressed to a variety of people; it is "sung" by both the sending and the receiving; and certainly it portrays the sense of superiority of the western Christian.

> Over the ocean wave, far, far away,
> There the poor heathen live, waiting for day;
> Groping in ignorance, dark as the night,
> No blessed Bible to give them the light.
>
> *Chorus:*
> Pity them, pity them, Christians at home,
> Haste with the bread of life, hasten and come.

Here in this happy land we have the light
Shining from God's own word, free, pure, and bright;
Shall we not send to them Bibles to read,
Teachers and preachers and all that they need?

Then, while the mission ship's glad tidings bring,
List! As that heathen band joyfully sing,
"Over the ocean wave, oh, see them come,
Bringing the bread of life, guiding us home."[12]

A very popular hymn, "From Greenland's Icy Mountains" (#8), was written in 1819 by Reginald Heber (1783–1826). Several years later Heber became the Bishop of Calcutta for the Anglican Church. He wrote hymns for use in his own church usually based on the Scriptures for the day's lectionary. Again in this hymn, as in the one above, is the assumption that those without Christ are calling for messengers "to deliver their land from error's chain" (see Acts 16:9). The second stanza is very pointed in its references to Ceylon's people and the evil of other religions. *The Methodist Hymnal* of 1935 eliminated this stanza. The third stanza has some sense of superiority regarding those "whose souls are lighted with wisdom from on high." The last stanza speaks of the hope for the world to be under the reign of God through Jesus, the Redeemer.

In the midst of these and other problematic hymns of the period, are found hymns that reflect the motivation of mission as being love, the hope for all to know Jesus without the threat of damnation, and a sense of praise and glory to God. Sir Edward Denny (1796–1889), a member of the Plymouth Brethren, wrote these words:

Come, blessed Lord, let every shore
And answering island sing
The praises of thy royal name,
And own thee as their King.[13]

William B. Collyer (1782–1854) was considered an "eloquent Evangelical preacher."[14] He wrote several hymns for missionary meetings. One of those is "Assembled at Thy Great Command." Collyer writes of mission as a calling and the spreading of truth. The third stanza lists some very specific petitions, while in the fourth stanza the "chosen heralds" are those who have gone out to spread the gospel. There is no mention of darkness, heathens, or pitying charity.

> Assembled at thy great command,
> Before thy face, dread King, we stand;
> The voice that marshaled every star
> Has called thy people from afar.
>
> We meet through distant lands to spread
> The truth for which the martyrs bled;
> Along the line, to either pole,
> The anthem of thy praise to roll.
>
> Our prayers assist; accept our praise;
> Our hopes revive; our courage raise;
> Our counsels aid; to each impart
> The single eye, the faithful heart.
>
> Forth with thy chosen herald come;
> Recall the wandering spirits home;
> From Zion's mount send forth the sound,
> To spread the spacious earth around.[15]

In 1872 Frances Ridley Havergal (1839–1879) wrote a simple, beautiful prayer asking for God's help in serving God. She first called it "A Worker's Prayer."[16] "Lord, Speak to Me" (#20) is about the need for God's presence within as one serves God. Havergal was very interested in mission and saw it as both proclaiming the gospel and living the gospel. The words "erring children" shows gentleness and love as does the idea of giving a hand to those that are troubled. She understands that the teacher must first learn in order to teach another. The last stanza expresses a total commitment to God. This hymn has been used at commissioning services for missionaries and deaconesses. It is in sharp contrast to many of the hymns of the earlier part of the nineteenth century.

It was an intense meeting when Marjorie, Louise, and Pastor Janice met to discuss Louise's paper. They raised hard questions with each other: "Was the gospel distorted by the missionary societies?" "Why did the hymns reflect the theology? Or did the hymns initiate the theology?" "Why did darkness come to imply sin?" "Was racism the real issue?" When they left Janice's office to go for coffee they all knew that their study had just touched the surface of the many issues. But they agreed to continue and meet again in a couple of months.

[1] Albert Edward Bailey, *The Gospel in Hymns* (New York: Charles Scribner's Sons, 1950), 52.

[2] David J. Bosch, *Transforming Mission* (Maryknoll, N.Y.: Orbis Books, 1991), 278-287.

[3] John Julian, *A Dictionary of Hymnology* (London: John Murray, Albemarle Street, 1907), 1226.

[4] *Hymns for the Use of the Methodist Episcopal Church* (New York: Carlton & Phillips, 1852), No. 976.

[5] *The Sabbath Hymn and Tune Book* (New York: Mason Brothers, Publishers, 1859), #1126.

[6] Paul J. Achtemeier, editor, *Harper's Bible Dictionary* (San Francisco: HarperSanFrancisco, 1985), 1166.

[7] *Hymnal of the Methodist Episcopal Church* (New York: Eaton & Mains, 1878), #925.

[8] Albert Edward Bailey, *The Gospel in Hymns* (New York: Charles Scribner's Sons, 1950), 493.

[9] Susan S. Tamke, *Make a Joyful Noise Unto the Lord* (Athens, Ohio: Ohio University Press, 1978), 131.

[10] David J. Bosch, *Transforming Mission* (Maryknoll, N.Y.: Orbis Books, 1991), 290.

[11] Ibid., 290.

[12] *The Evangelical Hymnal* (Harrisburg, Pa.: The Evangelical Publishing House, 1921), #417.

[13] *Hymnal of the Methodist Episcopal Church* (New York: Eaton & Mains, 1878), #914 stanza 2.

[14] John Julian, *A Dictionary of Hymnology* (London: John Murray, Albemarle Street, 1907), 243.

[15] *Hymnal of the Methodist Episcopal Church* (New York: Eaton & Mains, 1878), #922.

[16] Nicholas Smith, *Songs From the Hearts of Women* (Cambridge: University Press, 1903), 212.

CHAPTER 3

"The cup of water given for you still holds the freshness of your grace."

— Frank Mason North

arjorie and Louise were once again back in Pastor Janice's study. This time, their discussion centered on a small songbook Marjorie had found in her mother's things. The name in the book indicated that it might have belonged to a great aunt, but Marjorie wasn't sure. The book itself was of great interest. It was entitled "Marching Songs for Young Crusaders" and had been published by the Woman's Christian Temperance Union. There was no date on the book, but they guessed it would have been published shortly after the WCTU began in 1874. It contained songs encouraging children to abstain from drinking and to help rid the world of the "evil of drink."

> Oh, we are young Crusaders in the Army of the King!
> We'll shout and sing for temperance and we'll make
> the nation ring,
> We fight for Home Protection and the battle we shall win.
> The saloon shall surely go.[1]

This song and others had an obvious religious theme. The song was to be sung to the tune BATTLE HYMN OF THE REPUBLIC and small flags were to be waved by the children as they sang. It was written by Margaret B. Platt.

Mrs. L. G. McVean was the writer of another interesting song:

> Oh, give, yes, give, and look for the blessing,
>   You have the Savior's word;
> A meek and tender spirit possessing,
>   Be like your loving Lord.
>
> Give careful tho't and warm hands, to reach
>   The homes now spoiled by rum;
> Give bread to feed, and wisdom to teach them,
>   And gently bid them come.[2]

All this was fascinating, but the real question posed by Marjorie was, "Why this interest in temperance?" "Was there another shift in the understanding of mission during the last half of the nineteenth century?" Louise added a third question: "How did all this tie in with the Prohibition campaigns?"

Pastor Janice knew that somewhere in the midst of her books she had some things that might help with the questions. She just had to find the right books. She promised to send an email to each of them with some details and suggestions for further exploration. A couple of weeks later Pastor Janice came through with important information about the holiness movement, reforms, and the social gospel. Her email attachment summarized both as follows.

Holiness Movement and Reforms

John Wesley believed in justification by faith and the forgiveness of sin. He believed that sanctification or perfect love was available to everyone. Sometimes he called this Christian perfection, while others used the word "holiness." It involved an inner commitment to God and an outer expression of love for all neighbors. It was essential for the believer to love God with heart, mind, soul, and strength. It was also essential that the love of self be extended to the neighbor as an expression of God's love.

It was this belief in sanctification or Christian perfection that was the impetus for the holiness revivals that started in the 1830s in New England and continued through the end of the Civil War. John Wesley's understanding of holiness was part of the beliefs of the Methodist Episcopal Church, but during the period of revival the concept was expanded to include instant sanctification. This was promoted by Phoebe Palmer, a member of the Duane Street Methodist Episcopal Church (now Metropolitan Duane United Methodist Church) in New York City. She taught that anyone could give their all to Jesus and be completely consecrated to doing God's will and work.

This concept of holiness especially appealed to women, but also brought to the forefront some concerns. If women were to obey God it might mean they would have to speak in public, pray in mixed company, and even preach. All of these things and others were often denied women. Holiness gave women the religious assurance that they were of value, but it also put them into conflict with the mores of society. Holiness also motivated them to work for perfection in their homes, churches, and society.

Leonard Sweet says, when writing about what he calls the "Holiness Gene of Methodism":

> "Getting it right" is the hermeneutics of holiness—the embodiment of "perfect love" in history and the participation of changed lives in God's mission in the world. The fruit of justification is justice; grace issues in good works. Loved holiness is the synergy of faith and works moving the world from injustice to justice, from cruelty to compassion, from evil to good, from lies to truth. The holiness gene is more than an affair of the heart; justifying and sanctifying grace is an affair of public policy. Spreading scriptural holiness is habitually going about doing good, the "constant, zealous performance of all good works," the global transformation of the social, economic and political orders so that one can hear God say once again, as God said when the world was created, "it is good."....The inward journey of holiness concludes in the outward journey of justice.[3]

With the understanding that following God's will was essential and that holiness applied not only to the individual but also to societal issues, reform movements became very important. The concern for the abolition of slavery started early in the nineteenth century and continued through the Emancipation Proclamation. Women's rights, temperance, poverty, prostitution, and both foreign and home missions became the focus of many organizations. Women formed their own organizations around these concerns because they were not accepted in leadership roles in those formed by men. It was during the years immediately following the Civil War that the women's mission organizations in the major Protestant denominations were formed, as well as organizations dedicated to temperance and women's rights. In January 1868 the Woman's Foreign Missionary Society of New England was formed by Congregational women. In 1869 the

Woman's Foreign Missionary Society of the Methodist Episcopal Church was formed. By the end of the century there were over forty denominational women's missionary societies with emphasis on both work in the United States and in other countries.[4]

Social Gospel

At the same time reform movements were actively pursuing a better society, theologians were examining the concept of the reign (kingdom) of God. Some were advocating that the reign of God was a present reality while others felt it was only available in the future. During the years before and after the turn of the century the social gospel developed with its emphasis on a loving God, the concept of the "fatherhood of God and brotherhood of all people," the need for social reform, the concept of corporate sin and evil, and the present reality of the reign of God. Some people saw these ideas as anti-evangelism; some saw them as anti-Christ; some saw them as romantic. The proponents felt that to follow Christ was to be involved in redeeming the world and society. Those who believed in holiness and those who believed the tenets of the social gospel believed that the individual could gain perfection. It was the social gospel that preached that society could also be perfected.

Marjorie and Louise had a telephone conversation about Pastor Janice's email. They wanted to do more reading on both topics, but first they decided to look at some mission hymns of the period. They also agreed to look for stories about the hymns and some information about the authors. So, back they went to the collection of hymnals for more discoveries.

Abolition Hymns

A simple abolition hymn is "My Country" (#57) by an unknown author. The words are to be sung to the tune AMERICA. It is a plea for the end of slavery by paraphrasing some of the words in "My Country 'Tis of Thee" in a profound and appropriate way. The tying of the slave to the "tyrant's pride," the voice that calls "let all go free," and the understanding that purity comes with freedom—all speak for the abolition of slavery. The last stanza is a prayer for liberty. This can still be sung today since liberty is not secure for everyone.

Caroline Seward is the author of another abolition hymn. The text appeared in a hymnbook edited by Lowell Mason in 1859. In this hymn slavery, greed, and power are called sins. Current slavery is compared to the plight of the Hebrews in stanzas one and four. This is followed by the implication that God freed the Hebrews and thus can free the slaves of current times. This hymn can be sung to the tune OLD HUNDREDTH.

> Lord, when thine ancient people cried,
>   Oppressed and bound by Egypt's king,
> Thou didst Arabia's sea divide,
>   And forth thy fainting Israel bring.
>
> Lo! In these latter days, our land
>   Groans with the anguish of the slave!
> Lord God of hosts! Stretch forth thy hand,
>   Not shortened that it can not save.
>
> Roll back the swelling tide of sin,
>   The lust of gain, the lost of power;
> The day of freedom usher in:
>   How long delays th' appointed hour!
>
> As thou of old to Miriam's hand
>   The thrilling timbrel didst restore,
> And to her joyful song the land
>   Echoed from desert to the shore,
>
> Oh, let thy smitten ones again
>   Take up the chorus of the free:
> Praise ye the Lord! His power proclaim,
>   For he hath conquered gloriously![5]

Temperance Hymns

Temperance hymns were sung at rallies, parades, and in the schools. Some can be found in the denominational hymnals of the time. In the 1878 *Hymnal of the Methodist Episcopal Church* is a hymn by Edwin F. Hatfield (1803–1883). Hatfield was a clergyman of the Presbyterian Church and served churches in Missouri and New York City. He was a special agent of the Presbyterian Church to Union Theological

Seminary and also became the Stated Clerk of the Presbyterian General Assembly in 1846.[6] The hymn, "'Tis Thine Alone" speaks of the ruin that is brought by drinking. The drunkard is described as a captive "in bondage, heart and soul." The fourth stanza is a prayer for deliverance and the last stanza sees the cause of temperance as part of God's plan for saving the world.

'Tis thine alone, almighty Name,
 To raise the dead to life,
The lost inebriate to reclaim
 From passion's fearful strife.

What ruin hath intemperance wrought!
 How widely roll its waves!
How many myriads hath it brought
 To fill dishonored graves!

And see, O Lord, what numbers still
 Are maddened by the bowl,
Led captive at the tyrant's will
 In bondage, heart and soul.

Stretch forth thy hand, O God, our King,
 And break the galling chain;
Deliverance to the captive bring,
 And end the usurper's reign.

The cause of temperance is thine own;
 Our plans and efforts bless;
We trust, O Lord, in thee alone
 To crown them with success.[7]

One of the major concerns of the temperance movement was the destruction drink brought into the home. Men were the sole provider in most families, so when they drank the family income, the wife and children suffered for lack of food, shelter, and clothes. This concern caused the Woman's Christian Temperance Union to have as its motto: "For God and Home and Native Land." The WCTU believed that by eliminating access to liquor, men would provide for their families and thus improve the entire nation as well as the home.

This belief is stated in "Oh, Trust Ye in the Lord Forever" by Mary A. Lathbury (1841–1913). Lathbury was an associate editor of Sunday school materials for the Methodist Episcopal Church, writer of children's books, and a writer of poetry and hymns. She was an active participant in the WCTU. This hymn was in *The Methodist Protestant Church Hymnal* of 1901.

> Oh, trust ye in the Lord forever!
> > Strong is his arm and wide his love,
> He keepeth truth, he faileth never,
> > Tho' earth and sea and heav'n remove.
>
> *Chorus:*
> God is calling! He goes before us:
> > His strength is ours, his truth shall stand;
> Rise and follow, swell high the chorus,
> > For God, and home, and native land.
>
> Be strong, O men, who bear in battle
> > For us the banner and the shield;
> For strong to conquer, as to suffer,
> > Is he who leads you in the field.
>
> Lift up your eyes, O women, weeping
> > Besides your dead! The dawning day
> Has rent the seal of death forever,
> > And angels roll the stone away.
>
> Room for the right! Make room before us
> > For truth and righteousness to stand;
> And plant the holy banner o'er us;
> > "For God, and home, and native land."[8]

Missionary Society Hymns

The women's missionary societies were singing at every meeting. They sang the old songs, but they also picked up on the new ones that were published in small hymnals or in tracts. In 1888 E. S. Lorenz, a pastor in the United Brethren Church and then president of Lebanon Valley College in Pennsylvania, published the small hymnal *Missionary Songs*. In the preface he wrote:

In sending out this little collection of missionary songs, the editor has at last completed a little labor of love that has been planned for many years. Perhaps it would not even yet have been completed but for the urgent request of many of the good women who are engaged, among other important missionary labors, in training the missionary givers and workers of the twentieth century. That this little book may prove an efficient though very humble help in the consummation during that century of the grandest enterprise the ages have seen—the evangelization of the world—is the earnest desire of the editor.[9]

Among the songs were ones for children, those that encouraged giving, anthems for special services, and those appropriate to recruit workers. The latter included:

> Make me a worker for Jesus,
> Steadfast and earnest and true;
> Willing to do for the Master
> All he expects me to do.[10]

In "My Mission Field," the commitment of the worker to be led by Jesus is affirmed.

> I would toil in the field where he calleth me to go,
> Tho' humble my work may be;
> I would ask no more; I only care to know,
> 'Tis the way my Lord leadeth me.[11]

This little song about giving pennies encouraged children in their giving for mission:

> Hear the merry music ringing
> In the missionary box, in the missionary box;
> Shining pennies there are ringing
> Gospel music for the lands afar.[12]

A hymn written in 1869 was also popular in the missionary societies. Samuel Wolcott (1813–1886) was a Congregational pastor serving in Cleveland, Ohio, when he wrote "Christ for the World We Sing" (#6). He had been a missionary in Syria for a short time and while in

Ohio, served as the secretary of the Ohio Home Missionary Society. This hymn was developed from the motto of the YMCA in Ohio: "Christ for the World, and the World for Christ."[13] The theme of the hymn is to bring the world to Christ, but to do so out of the motivation of love and with "fervent prayer." Unity with those who receive the message is highlighted in the third stanza. Throughout the hymn the emphasis is on all who do not know Jesus, not just on those who are in another place or country.

"Rescue the Perishing" (#70) was also written in 1869. The hymn came from Fanny Crosby's (1820–1915) experiences of working with the poor and oppressed in New York City. It soon became a motivator of home mission activity throughout the country. Fanny Crosby was a writer of over 8,500 hymns. She became blind as an infant, taught for years in the New York School for the Blind, was a lifelong Methodist, and a tireless worker in the city missions of New York City. The rescuer, as indicated in the hymn, is to care, weep, lift up, plead, be loving and kind, and tell of Jesus. This can be done because "duty demands it," but also because "strength for thy labor the Lord will provide." As the chorus proclaims, Jesus does the saving.

"We've a Story to Tell to the Nations" (#74) was written by H. Ernest Nichol (1862–1926), an English musician and poet. This hymn was written in 1896 and became very popular. There is within it some of the superiority feelings of earlier hymns and a sense that the story, the song, and the Savior are owned by the singer. Even so, the hymn speaks of a story full of truth, mercy, peace, and light that is available to everyone. In the second stanza is the plea that the song shall "shatter the spear and sword" and bring peace to the world. In the last stanza the universality of Christ is expressed. The tune is lively and fun to sing which may be one of the reasons it has endured. This hymn was the theme song in 1924 of the Girl's Auxiliary of the Southern Baptist Woman's Missionary Union.[14]

Home missions became a focus of work as the reform movements grew within the United States. Concern was expressed and programs established for the ex-slaves, for the poor immigrants coming to the United States from many European countries, for the miners and their families in Appalachia, and the workers brought in to build the railroads.

Perhaps the greatest home missionary hymn is "Where Cross the Crowded Ways of Life" (#67) written by Frank Mason North (1850–1935) in 1903. North was a Methodist clergyman serving churches in Connecticut until 1892. In that year he became the corresponding secretary of the New York Church Extension and Missionary Society (now the New York City Society of The United Methodist Church). He held that position until 1912 when he became the corresponding secretary of the Board of Foreign Missions of the Methodist Episcopal Church.[15] He was in that important position until he retired in 1924, and knew extensively both the home and foreign mission work of the Methodist Church and the ecumenical community.

North not only preached the social gospel, he lived it in his work for the urban poor. The hymn is a powerful expression of what he experienced in the city and what he believed about the responsibility of every Christian.

Stanza 1: In the midst of the racial and cultural cries and the noise of those seeking personal gain one can hear the voice of Jesus.

Stanza 2: The tears of Christ are seen in the "wretchedness and need" and in "the lures of greed."

Stanza 3: Christ is present with the child, the woman, and the man who have needs and can find comfort only in the heart of Christ.

Stanza 4: Social service and salvation is combined as the "cup of water" given in the name of Jesus. Christ's gift of grace is offered as well.

Stanza 5: A prayer for Jesus to come into the city to heal and walk with the "restless."

Stanza 6: All must love and serve as Christ did until the "city of our God" comes.

Frank Mason North was asked to write "Where Cross the Crowded Ways of Life" by the Methodist hymnal committee because they had few modern missionary hymns for the 1905 hymnal. North said of the hymn:

> It is an expression of the tremendous movement of the soul of the Gospel in our times which demands that the follower of Christ must make the interest of the people his own, and must find the heart of the world's need if he is in any way to represent his Master among men.[16]

Laura Scherer Copenhaver (1868–1940) was a leader in mountain missionary work in the United Lutheran Church in America. She was also a professor of English literature at Marion College in Virginia.[17] In 1915 she wrote "Heralds of Christ" (#64) for a summer mission conference. She says: "I was moved with a deep sense of unity with the builders of the King's Highway in far lands, next door to me in America, and even with those great ones I had known as a child now gone on with the immortals by way of Africa and India."[18]

The hymn is a challenge to those who carry the tidings of Jesus to do so swiftly and in all places. The highway could be a metaphor for the reign of God or the missionary movement. The last stanza sees a world without war led by the Prince of Peace. In 1934 Copenhaver wrote an article about this hymn in which she said:

> Today in every land Christians are uniting to build a Kingdom which shall have no geographical bounds, no limitations of race, no barriers of caste or class. Many feet are on the Highway today. Many hands are building. Not all are using the same tools or the same tempo, but all are building with their eyes fixed on the same leader, Jesus Christ. There are many roads, but no matter whether they stretch over mountain or river, through open plains or dark jungle, the Highway will be firm and straight because it reaches to one goal, the Kingdom of God.[19]

Marjorie and Louise were encouraged by these more recent mission hymns. They could connect with them. At the monthly meeting of United Methodist

Women, they shared some of their findings and learnings. The women were very interested and Hazel, a woman in her nineties, invited Louise to come to her home the next week to review some old papers she had kept from her early days in "the missionary society." Once again Louise went off to do more research. She then shared her findings with Marjorie and Pastor Janice.

Hymns Used in National Missionary Organizations and Meetings

At each meeting of the national missionary organizations related to what is now known as United Methodist Women, hymns were sung. In the early days the titles were in the minutes of the meetings or sometimes the hymn number was indicated. In 1889 in the Woman's Board of Mission of the Methodist Episcopal Church, South they sang "Jesus Shall Reign" and "From Greenland's Icy Mountains." Both of these hymns were popular in the meetings in the 1880s and 1890s. By 1938, in what then was known as the General Missionary Council of the same church, "Jesus Shall Reign" was sung twice with "Heralds of Christ" also included in a time of worship.

In 1888 at the 7th Annual Meeting of the Woman's Home Missionary Society of the Methodist Episcopal Church, a hymn by Mary A. Lathbury was introduced. It appears to have been commissioned for use by the organization. Lathbury was a Methodist laywoman and writer of two familiar hymns: "Day Is Dying in the West" and "Break Thou the Bread of Life." She was a strong supporter of missions. The hymn is entitled "The Coming of the King." Stanzas 1 and 4-6 are printed below:

> O make ready for the King,
> And prepare your offering;
> For His coming, swiftly dawning
> Breaks around us like the morning;
> And our eyes may catch the grace
> Of the glory of His face,
> Bringing light unto the world.
>
> Alleluia! Christ is born!
> And the world rolls past its morn.

Heaven pours the tender glory
Of Redemption's wondrous story,
With its deeps of love and pain,
With its heights of loss and gain,
    Through a woman to the world.

Alleluia! Christ is risen!
Angels at His rended prison,
Radiant with His passing glory,
Send the resurrection story,
Winged with peace to conquer strife,
Bearing everlasting life,
    Through a woman to the world.

Alleluia! Christ is King!
Wide His palace portals fling!
Forth in fair procession flowing
Come the royal daughters, going
Where the King Himself may send
Love and life that hath no end,
    Through a woman to the world.[20]

This hymn calls for women to prepare for Jesus, the bringer of light into the world. Then the story of Jesus is told from a feminist perspective. It was "through a woman that Christ" was born and the Resurrection story told. In the last stanza "the royal daughters" will go where Christ sends them to share His love "through a woman to the world."

In 1913, Fannie E. Heck (1862–1915) wrote a similar hymn for the Southern Baptist Woman's Missionary Union. She served as national president of the organization from 1892 until 1915. In "The Woman's Hymn" Heck urges women to be active in mission work and receive Christ's crown of light. June Hadden Hobbs says this about the hymn:

> In these stanzas, Heck calls upon the bonds of shared woman-hood. Other Christian women are her "sisters" even if they live in other countries; she celebrates their motherhood by inviting them to "come, clasping children's hands."…Heck presents an apocalyptic vision in which women lead a new order of Christians into a triumphant era.[21]

Heck encourages women to "work with your courage high" and be upheld by the love of Christ which is the motivation for mission. The last stanza is an assurance of "joy evermore." This hymn is sung to ITALIAN HYMN.

Come, women, wide proclaim
Life through your Savior slain;
Sing evermore.
Christ, God's effulgence bright,
Christ, Who arose in might,
Christ, Who crowns you with light,
Praise and adore.

Come, clasping children's hands,
Sisters from many lands,
Teach to adore.
For the sin sick and worn,
The weak and overborne,
All who in darkness mourn,
Pray, work, yet more.

Work with your courage high,
Sing of the daybreak nigh,
Your love outpour.
Stars shall your brow adorn,
Your heart leap with the morn,
And by His Love upborne,
Hope and adore.

Then when the garnered field
Shall to our Master yield
A bounteous store,
Christ, hope of all the meek,
Christ, Whom all the earth shall seek,
Christ your reward shall speak,
Joy evermore.[22]

After the 1939 formation of The Methodist Church the women's organization was called the Woman's Society of Christian Service with an official publication, *The Methodist Woman*. Periodically there appeared in the magazine hymns for use in the local and conference units as well as entire worship services with suggested hymns.

In the November 1945 issue, "Peace Through His Cross" (#26) by Catherine Baker (1879–1972), a missionary to China and Korea, was printed. In this hymn, written at the end of World War II, there is thankfulness for peace, for the love of Christ, and for the reconciling power that comes through the cross. The second stanza is a call for women to pray, speak out, and give healing to those who suffer because of the war. The last stanza expresses a hope for world understanding, brotherhood, and the end to hatred.

The magazine also carried suggestions for music to be used in the mission education of the organization. Music was not to be seen as an "add-on," but a vital part of the worship experiences. New hymns were to be introduced and the older hymns used when appropriate to the topic of the meeting. In work with children, music was to be used as a means of education, motivation, and to create an excitement about mission. "Jesus Belongs to All Children" (#17) was published in 1939 and written by Alice Jean Cleator. This hymn helps children understand that Jesus is for all children. Note the comparisons: between this country and others afar, between countries of snow and of flowers, among the various colors of children, and between cottage and palace. Children are encouraged to "send the glad tidings away" and to help make Jesus known.

In the September 1949 issue of *The World Evangel*, the magazine of the Women's Society of World Service of the Evangelical United Brethren Church, was found a prayer poem by Bessie Porter Head (1850–1936). It is a plea for passion to give, to go, and to pray for the world.

> Stir me, oh stir me, Lord! I care not how;
> But stir my heart in passion for the world.
> Stir me to give, to go—but most to pray.
> Stir till Thy blood-red banner be unfurled
> O'er lands that still in deepest darkness lie
> O'er deserts where no cross is lifted high.[23]

At the 2nd Assembly of the Woman's Society of Christian Service[24] in 1946, the theme was "He Is Our Peace" and the theme hymn was

"Come! Peace of God" (#7) by May Rowland (1870–1959). The hymn was written in 1928 during the time of unrest between the two world wars.[25] The hymn is a prayer for peace. Images of war are strong in stanza two with the phrases "weapon forged in fires of hate" and "fields of strife lie desolate and bare." Hatred and selfishness are put in opposition to peace, brotherhood, and love. The last stanza identifies that peace must "rule within our hearts" for there to be peace in the world.

The 5th Assembly in 1958 had the theme "Christ's Message for Today" with "Eternal God, Whose Power Upholds" (#35) as the theme song. This hymn was written by Henry Hallam Tweedy (1868–1953) in 1929 upon the call of the Hymn Society of America for new mission hymns. He was a Congregational minister serving churches until 1903 when he became a professor of Practical Theology at Yale Divinity School.[26] God is portrayed as a God of love, truth, beauty, righteousness, and power in the hymn. It is because of God that the people of the world are brought together. In the second stanza the prayer is "to spread Thy gracious reign" so that greed and hate shall be stopped by kindness and peace. The prayer in the third stanza is for wisdom to replace ignorance and in the fourth stanza ugliness is to be replaced with beauty and loveliness. The last stanza is a prayer for inspiration for those who are the "heralds of good news."

"Many Gifts, One Spirit" (#69) was written by Al Carmines (1936–2005) for the 1974 Assembly of United Methodist Women. A United Church of Christ minister, Carmines wrote many hymns, musicals, and plays. This hymn emphasizes unity in the midst of diversity, fear that can be "cast out" by love, an uncertain future made holy by the Giver, and praise to God as the source of many gifts.

In the 1998 Assembly the theme song was "Make Plain the Vision" (#50) by Shirley Erena Murray (b. 1931). Murray is a Presbyterian laywoman from New Zealand. Her hymn helped the gathering address the issues of God's vision of justice, wholeness, and love. In the first stanza she calls on God to inspire, to give wisdom for "a vision we dare not resist." She then asks the hard question about "who will be the midwife to justice and peace?" The chorus puts it directly in the hands, hearts, and power of each follower of Jesus. The second and third stanzas explain more fully the responsibility to lead, to serve, to stay "tuned to our time," and to live a vision that "the world will believe." The music to this hymn was composed by Carlton R. Young (b. 1926), the editor of *The United Methodist Hymnal* of 1989.

Once again Louise, Marjorie, and Pastor Janice were amazed and enriched by all they had learned, read, and sung. Louise regaled them with her memories of the Assemblies she had attended during the last twenty plus years. They agreed further conversation was going to be needed about the theology of the hymns, an understanding of mission today, and the responsibility of each participant in God's mission. Marjorie was going to be gone over spring break and Louise was involved in the local school board election, so they decided to wait a couple of months for the next phase of their journey.

[1] *Marching Songs for Young Crusaders* (Chicago: Woman's Temperance Publishing Association), 5.

[2] Ibid., 47.

[3] Leonard Sweet, *11 Genetic Gateways to Spiritual Awakening* (Nashville: Abingdon Press, 1998), 143, 146.

[4] Dana L. Robert, *American Women in Mission* (Macon, Ga.: Mercer University Press, 1997), 129.

[5] *The Sabbath Hymn and Tune Book* (New York: Mason Brothers, Publishers, 1859), #1104.

[6] John Julian, *A Dictionary of Hymnology* (London: John Murray, Albemarle Street, 1907), 495-496.

[7] *Hymnal of the Methodist Episcopal Church* (New York: Eaton & Mains, 1878), No. 895.

[8] *The Methodist Protestant Church Hymnal* (Baltimore and Pittsburgh: Board of Publication of the Methodist Protestant Church, 1902), No. 528.

[9] E. S. Lorenz, *Missionary Songs* (Dayton, Ohio: W. J. Shuey, Publisher, 1888), 2.

[10] Ibid., "Make Me A Worker for Jesus," #14.

[11] Ibid., "My Mission Field," #15.

[12] Ibid., "Missionary Music," #22.

[13] Kenneth W. Osbeck, *Amazing Grace* (Grand Rapids, Mich.: Kregel Publications, 2002), 35.

[14] June Hadden Hobbs, *"I Sing for I Cannot Be Silent"* (Pittsburgh, Pa.: University of Pittsburgh Press, 1997), 140.

[15] His position today is called General Secretary, General Board of Global Ministries of The United Methodist Church.

[16] E. E. Ryden, *Christian Hymnody* (Rock Island, Ill.: Augustana Press, 1959), 588.

[17] Carlton R. Young, *Companion to The United Methodist Hymnal* (Nashville: Abingdon Press), 734.

[18] Robert Guy McCutchan, *Our Hymnody* (Nashville: Abingdon Press, 1937), 466-467.

[19] Ibid., 467.

[20] Minutes of the Woman's Home Missionary Society, Methodist Episcopal Church, 1888.

[21] June Hadden Hobbs, *"I Sing for I Cannot Be Silent"* (Pittsburgh, Pa.: University of Pittsburgh Press, 1997), 139.

[22] *The Cyberhymnal* (http://www.cyberhymnal.org)

[23] *The World Evangel* (September 1949).

[24] Assemblies are quadrennial events held for the membership of United Methodist Women. They are non-legislative and provide challenge, inspiration, and fellowship. In the Evangelical United Brethren Church similar events were called Quadrennial Conventions.

[25] Robert Guy McCutchan, *Our Hymnody* (Nashville: Abingdon Press, 1937), 489.

[26] Albert Edward Bailey, *The Gospel in Hymns* (New York: Charles Scribner's Sons, 1950), 575-576.

CHAPTER 4

*"Jesu, Jesu, fill us with your love,
show us how to serve the
neighbors we have from you."*

— Tom Colvin

his time it was Louise who called Marjorie and Pastor Janice to meet at her house on Saturday afternoon. Louise had just been elected to the school board so she was learning everything she could about the governance concerns of the district. She was excited about serving on the school board, but she still had some new ideas about music and mission. She had found in recent professional music magazines some interesting discussions regarding ethnomusicology. She explained to the other two that ethnomusicology, defined simply, is the study of the music and musical practices of a particular people. It also studies the role of music within the day-to-day life of a people. Louise wanted their discussion of mission music to be broadened to include the music that went with the missionary and that which developed from within the culture served.

Pastor Janice rolled her eyes knowing that this was going to be a much longer journey than she had imagined. Marjorie blinked, but then jumped right in suggesting talking to a couple of recently retired missionaries she knew in another church. At least, she thought, they would know something about the music they used and what was sung in the churches. She also wondered aloud about the music used in the Korean and Hispanic churches in the United States.

Finally the three came up with a plan:

* Louise would do the work on ethnomusicology and its role in mission;
* Marjorie would talk to the two missionaries she knew and others that they might introduce to her; and
* Pastor Janice would feed to each of them articles and other resources that might help in their study. She had some things from a couple of musicians she had met through the years and some former missionaries.

They agreed to keep each other posted via email and attach occasional summary papers. These papers are collected below.

Early Missionaries and Music

When missionaries were sent to serve they took with them their Bible and their hymnbook. Most would have taken the denominational hymnal currently in use in their home church. After 1875 many would have also taken with them Sunday school hymnals and/or gospel hymnals published by such people as Ira D. Sankey, Philip Bliss, or Homer Rodeheaver. For example, the first missionaries of the Woman's Foreign Missionary Society, Methodist Episcopal Church, were sent to India in 1869. Most likely Isabella Thoburn and Clara Swain took with them *Hymns for the Use of the Methodist Episcopal Church*, revised in 1852. It was a small book—about 3" x 5" x 2"—fitting easily into a corner of a suitcase. The hymns they knew from that hymnal were those by Charles Wesley, Isaac Watts, Anne Steele, James Montgomery, and others. These were the hymns that would be translated into the indigenous languages, either by them or others.

In the section on "Missions, Foreign" in the 1907 edition of *A Dictionary of Hymnology*, a detailed listing of hymns and hymnals published in various languages and dialects is given for most of the Protestant missions around the world. The author, W. R. Stevenson, says:

> Most persons have some idea of the great work accomplished by Christian missionaries in the translation of the Holy Scriptures into almost all known languages; but few have ever thought how much has been done by them in the translation and composition of hymns, the preparation of hymn-books, and in general, in the introduction of Christian Hymnody among the various nations to whom they have preached the Gospel.[1]

Many missionaries would translate the hymns they knew into the language of the people. They ran into difficulty with syllables and accents, with rhythm in tunes, with rhyming, and with the translation of some words. Other missionaries would attempt to write simple words in the language of the people and set the words to a tune from the missionary's home country. In some countries congregational singing was difficult due to a variety of local customs that did not allow men and women to sing together or the practice of religious leaders of other faiths not allowing the people to sing.

The music of the people was often extremely hard for the missionaries to understand or appreciate. It was so foreign to their western style music, that some even called it "a work of the devil." Others felt that indigenous music would be inappropriate for Christian poetry. Mary L. Cort, a Presbyterian missionary to Siam, wrote this, in the early years of the twentieth century, about the music of that country:

> Native airs have not yet been utilized in Christian song. Siamese music is very weird and monotonous, and is never used in the temple services, only at funerals and weddings, in processions, and in connection with boat races and theatres. Every native song is composed in lines of 11 syllables, but the Siamese learn western tunes readily, and seem to like them, especially tunes in 11's metre, and everything in a minor key.[2]

William Carey probably translated the first hymn into an Indian language around 1798. Sixty years later in India hymns were being written in the indigenous languages using indigenous tunes by missionaries and converts. The various denominations with missions in India developed their own hymnals or shared depending on the language.

> Generally it is noted in India that with the progress of years the use of English metres and tunes has been increasingly superseded by that of metres and tunes belonging to the country, which have come down to our time unwritten, but have been long used in festivals, at weddings and the like.[3]

Stevenson closes his twenty-page discussion by saying:

> The languages and dialects in which Christian hymns in connection with Foreign Missions have been written, or into which they have been translated, are nearly 150, and that in many of them, several hymn books of considerable

size have been prepared....All these by the energy and diligence of Christian missionaries have been mastered, their words have been arranged in tuneful measures, and in them God's praises are now sung, and His wonderful works declared.[4]

In Africa the missionaries of the nineteenth and early twentieth centuries could not accept the drums and the dancing of the people. Drums were outlawed in the churches as a symbol of the heathen nature of the people. Many missionaries also felt that the indigenous tunes and African instruments were inappropriate due to their use in spirit worship or other "heathen" activities. Instead some missionaries had hauled in on the backs of porters, pianos or pump organs to provide music for the church using European tunes. They translated the hymns they knew and the people learned to sing them, but the "tone languages" of the people could not be translated and the hymns thus had little or no meaning.

Tom Colvin (1925–2000), a Scottish Presbyterian missionary to Malawi, told the following story about hymns and hymn writing in Malawi during the early missionary days.

> In 1875 a group of missionaries from Scotland together with a few African evangelists from Lovedale in South Africa landed from a boat on Lake Malawi at a place they called Cape Maclear. This was the planting of the Church in Malawi which has grown continuously since then. Soon, the Mission moved to the north of the lake and became established amongst the Ngoni, a warrior tribe which had migrated earlier from Swaziland.
>
> The Ngoni had settled and inter-married with other tribes as a result of which they had lost much of their culture and even much of their language. Only the old ones could still speak Chi Ngoni. One attribute of their culture remained—their love of music and in particular, singing. What a blessing it was that the one who was charged to take the Gospel to them was William Koyi, the leading South African evangelist, who was of the same language group and culture as themselves. He understood them and was accepted by them. He taught

the Gospel in song, using Zulu and Ngoni melodies from the old days, south of the Great River, the Zambezi.

In the following years, from about 1880, great musicians emerged, writing new Christian hymns to old melodies of war-songs, love-songs, work-songs, praise-songs and laments....The result of this early interest was that from the very birth of Christianity among the Ngoni it was accepted as natural and desirable that they should create their own Church music.

Sadly, the encouragement of hymn-making to African melodies did not continue for long. Later missionaries were not interested. Their main interest was to introduce European hymns, however inappropriate, to European tunes, however unsingable....It seemed that indigenous hymn-writing had come to an end because of lack of interest by missionaries.

Fortunately, about 1900 a new missionary arrived amongst the Ngoni with a more liberal view. He was Donald Fraser from Scotland. As soon as he had mastered the languages he turned his attention to the hymns. He actively encouraged the composition of indigenous church hymns. It was Fraser who enthused Mawelero Tembo and others to use the old melodies and write new Christian words to them. Fraser went on to organize great conventions for hymn singing at which new hymns were welcomed. At some of these as many as fifty new hymns were performed. With Fraser's encouragement, the inherent Ngoni love of music and com-position flourished to the benefit of the whole Church and the strengthening of the missionary movement. Many of these songs were used in teaching the faith as the most appropriate way for a mainly non-literate people to learn and remember. Other songs were on themes of topical importance e.g. against polygamy, or in favor of education, while many were evangelical appeals such as were common from missionaries....Fraser and others found no difficulty in appreciating this mixture of the old and the new. They recognized that the inherent African love of music should be encouraged as a channel for expressing the emerging Christian faith.[5]

After reading the story about Malawi, Louise remembered a hymn written by Tom Colvin. She encouraged the others to find it in their hymnals. She suggested they use it as a devotional reading while they continued to work on their "assignments."

"Jesu, Jesu" (#16) was written in 1969 by Tom Colvin for a meeting of evangelists in Ghana. The music is a folk tune from Ghana and the words are about loving the neighbor no matter his or her status. This hymn suggests that followers of Christ are to "kneel at the feet of our friends" as did Jesus when he washed the feet of the disciples.

Tom Colvin believed in using tunes of the people to proclaim the story of Jesus. He often took the tunes of women's work songs and added Christian words for use in workshops, Sunday school, or worship services. Some of his songs were in English for use in English language services in schools or churches or at times when participants did not know each other's language, but did know English. Colvin was not a musician by training. He described himself as "a church worker who wrote hymns to African tunes out of necessity in my work."[6] "Come, Let Us Seek Our God's Protection" (#63) is a Malawian folk song, collected from the women at Chilema, Malawi. It is a faith teaching song for use of the church in Malawi. It is sung with a leader doing the stanzas and the entire group singing the refrain. It is simple and words can be added as appropriate for the service or class.

Ethnomusicology and Mission

During the twentieth century things did begin to change regarding the use of indigenous music in worship. Some of the change came about because of missionaries like Tom Colvin, who, out of necessity, in their teaching and preaching incorporated words and music in the "language" of the people. Some of the change came because trained musicians serving as missionaries were able to transcribe indigenous tunes and appreciated a variety of musical systems. Other changes came as ethnomusicologists raised the consciousness of mission leaders about the value of using the people's musical forms within worship and Christian Education.

Bliss Wiant (1895–1975) and Mildred Wiant (1898–2001) were missionaries to China for the Methodist Episcopal Church from 1923 to 1951. Bliss Wiant was ordained with a master's degree in hymnology and became a part of the music department at Yenching University in Peiping. Mildred was a trained musician and teacher of voice. Wiant took with him to China an appreciation of cross-cultural music and its potential use in worship. As he was teaching the western classic religious music to his choirs and preparing them for concerts, he was also working with T. C. Chao, Dean of the School of Religion at the university. They worked together in translating western hymns and in preparing a hymnbook of Chinese folk songs with simple verses by Chao for use in Bible storytelling. This collection was published in 1931 as *Christian Fellowship Hymns*. Wiant wrote in July 1932:

> The first edition of the hymnbook was sold out in ten months. We now have revised and enlarged it and have the manuscript well on the way towards a second edition. It makes an appeal to college students and to people of that rank...I have heard of other people who are now getting interested in this type of work and are planning similar publications—the more the better for the cause.[7]

Chen Zemin in writing about this hymnal sixty-five years later said: "Chao's hymnal marked an important attempt to incorporate indigenous culture into Christian hymn writing with his beautiful, creative poetic expression of Christian spirituality; the result was a plain and easy-to-sing vernacular style."[8]

Bliss Wiant also served on the first union hymnal committee of the Methodist Episcopal Church, North and South, the Church of Christ in China (which included the Presbyterian and 15 other denominations), the Episcopal Church of China, the Northern Baptist Church, and the Congregational Church. He prepared new Chinese tunes for fifty original hymns included in that hymnal and edited 450 other tunes for the book. This hymnal, *Hymns of Universal Praise*, was published in 1935.

> Never in the history of hymnology have such divergent communions worked harmoniously together on such a

fundamental issue as that of providing hymns for the people. This is a witness to the fact that Christianity in China has a unity of purpose and action not known in the history of denominational Christendom.[9]

The hymn, "Zhi ran fu yu hua tu shi" ("Lord, for Thy Revealing Gifts") (#71) is from that hymnal. Bliss Wiant wrote:

> This tune dates back into many hundreds of years before Christ. It was known and loved by Confucius, 500 B.C. It has been used up to the present as an instrumental solo, the instrument on which it was played being known as the "Ancient Lute"–it has seven strings and is the oldest instrument known to the Chinese. The name of this piece means "In a Happy Mood."
>
> To use music of this kind in Christian worship as a hymn tune is a new departure for China. Inasmuch as the tune has had such a long life and has happy and noble associations, it is hoped that this experiment will prove successful. Such music is thoroughly consonant with the best in Chinese culture and background and as such should make a permanent contribution to the enrichment of hymnology in the Christian Church.[10]

One of T. C. Chao's (1888–1979) hymns, "Rise to Greet the Sun" (#27), was translated by the Wiants. It is a morning prayer praising God for the sun, birds, and flowers in the first stanza. God is asked for good conduct to help the child, youth, and aged during a day of service in stanza two. The last stanza is thanks for "glad cotton coat, plain food satisfies" and all else that God supplies. This hymn tune was first heard by Wiant in a marketplace being played by a street musician on a flute. Only the melody should be sung as is true of many Asian melodies.[11]

T. Janet Surdam (1912–1990) arrived in China in 1939 as a missionary of the Woman's Society of Christian Service. She was assigned to the Methodist School and Church in Pishan as a music and Christian Education teacher. She wrote many bilingual songs, first in Chinese and then in English. She found the "Chinese language, with its tonal qualities and beautiful rhythms, ideal for music" and intentionally tried to fit the music and the tones of the language together. She wrote often for children and used simple poetry and Scripture so that memorization would be easy.[12]

Surdam was jailed in China during the Communist revolution for 200 days from 1949 to 1950. During that time she wrote many hymns in her head, memorized them, and when released, put them on paper. One of those hymns is "This Is the Day" (#45), written on Epiphany 1950. It is based on Psalm 118 and is a song of thanksgiving in the midst of great hardship. This hymn was printed in the November 1977 issue of *Response* and used in various programming endeavors of the Women's Division.

After World War II and the subsequent liberation struggles that took place in many parts of the world, missionaries and mission leaders became more open to indigenous hymns, tunes, and instruments within worship. They were willing to experiment with tunes and simple words and soon learned that many of the people appreciated the efforts. In some locales the use of indigenous instruments, drums, and tunes brought new people into the church. No longer was the music "foreign" to the new believer, thus people were more accepting of Christianity. In some large city churches though, the missionaries had done such a good job of teaching the western hymns and music that the worshippers did not consider their own music as Christian and were unwilling to sing such in worship. This understanding still exists today in many places in Asia and the Caribbean where Christians prefer translated western hymns over music from their own culture in formal worship services.

In the 1960s in the Philippines, Delbert Rice and Elena Maquiso separately worked with minority tribes to develop truly indigenous songs. Rice was a missionary of the Evangelical United Brethren Church working with the United Church of Christ in the Philippines. Maquiso was on the faculty at Silliman University in the Philippines. They used a step-by-step method in their work including:

* a complete analysis of the musical culture of the people;
* determining if any of the music could be adapted for use as Christian music with a hard look at how the tune had been previously used; and then
* the actual writing, evaluation, and testing of an indigenous hymn in the language of the tribe.

This was a long process, but proved successful and encouraged others to do likewise.[13] Their method started with the basics of ethnomusicology.

Elena Maquiso (b. 1914) is the writer and composer of "This Land of Beauty Has Been Given" (#49). This is a mission hymn about justice regarding the land, about broken relationships brought about by selfishness and bitterness, about the dreams of a farmer for his family, and about the necessity of the rich to share their land with the poor for "the right to land is for us all."

It took many years for mission leaders to understand that the gospel is not limited to one culture. Even the early Christians had a difficult time with the concept that the Gentiles did not need to be circumcised to be Christian. Slowly, with the insistence at times of those desiring to make the gospel their own, the music and worship within the worldwide church is expressing the entire "language" of a specific group of people. Pablo Sosa (b. 1933), a Methodist pastor, musician, and teacher in Argentina, shares this wonderful story:

> When the Christian missionaries arrived in the Chaco area in northern Argentina, they were warmly received by the mild and peaceful Qom people, who easily accepted this loving new Son of God, Jesus Christ, even if they did not quite understand why he had to suffer such a cruel death. Were people actually so evil in Jesus Christ's world? When the time came to think of the new generations, they prepared themselves for the big feast. And the missionaries watched in horror as their new converts engaged in an all night long sexual orgy where lusty songs and dances were accompanied by the shrieking sound of a tin can violin with only one string. They (the missionaries) had never heard of communal

marriage feasts, common to many aboriginal societies. They only knew of the bridegroom waiting for his bride while she walked down the aisle at the sound of the organ. Anything else was worldly, pagan, or devilish and should be abolished, uprooted, annihilated.

The Qom people were not happy about it, but they accepted the edict to destroy all tin can violins and never again sing or dance their music. They thanked God that those nice people from abroad had come to warn them that their old ways of life had been inherited from the devil, and to teach them such beautiful new songs, totally different from their old shrieking ones, so sweetly accompanied by the harmonium.

When the ethnomusicologist came through the Chaco area, and with her recording machine in hand asked a venerable old man to sing one of their songs, she was appalled to hear him sing "Jesus Loves Me, This I Know," and furthermore he vehemently refused to sing any of the songs they sang "before knowing the Lord." The article she wrote for the academic magazine told about the devastation of the aboriginal cultures made by foreign Protestant missionaries.

Time went by and the new winds of the inculturation of the Gospel blew over the Chaco when teachers and students from the Protestant Theological Institute, ISEDET, came in contact with the Qom people. Long hours of conversation (actually patiently waiting in silence for somebody to speak) brought about painfully the story of the violin, the songs, the dances, and the difficulty to believe that all this is given to you by God, not the devil. And then the search in the deepest jungle for someone who still remembered how to build a Qom violin. And the faces of the young people as they dared to begin assembling their instruments, re-discovering old songs, writing new ones. Finally playing and singing openly what had been banned for so many years. The reconciliation took place within them of their ancient culture and the new life in Christ.[14]

Pablo Sosa writes hymns, poetry, and liturgy. Among his many hymns is "El cielo canta" ("Heaven Is Singing") (#56). This hymn was written in 1958 but became meaningful in the 1970s as Argentina experienced difficult political unrest. He found himself standing in solidarity with the poor and oppressed of his country and to sing this hymn with its folk style "became a way of living out his faith." "Teaching this hymn was not only a means of sharing a song of joy within the Christian context, but a mission to help those who sang it understand the poverty and suffering of the people represented by this musical style."[15] The hymn declares that all lives are full of God's glory, united in love, and always willing to bear witness to God.

I-to Loh (b. 1936) served as a missionary of The United Methodist Church from 1982 to 1994 at the Asian Institute for Liturgy and Music in Manila, Philippines. Loh was a professor of church music and ethnomusicology at that institution as well as at Tainan Theological College in Taiwan. He later became president of Tainan. Loh is probably the only ethnomusicologist that has served as a missionary of The United Methodist Church. His work is highly regarded throughout Asia and in the area of worship and liturgy, by the ecumenical community. He also served as the general editor in 1990 and 2000 of *Sound the Bamboo*, the hymnal of the Christian Conference of Asia. In writing about the first edition of this hymnal, C. Michael Hawn said:

> Many Asian Christians have felt that they have had to make a choice between Christianity and Asian culture. The publication of an Asian hymnal, notated as nearly as possible in a manner that encourages an authentic presentation of the songs, is not just the work of an ethnomusicologist who specializes in church music. It is a theological endeavor designed to help Asian Christians find their cultural voice in the context of Christian liturgy.[16]

For the 8th General Assembly of the Christian Conference of Asia in 1985, I-to Loh wrote "Jesus Christ Sets Free to Serve" (#5) as the theme song. It is based on Luke 4:18-19 and calls for followers of Christ to be "partners in God's mission." It is Jesus that makes us free to love and to struggle for "the fullness of life." The last phrase is a prayer for God's help as we care, share, and bear each other's burden.

Hymns have been translated and music transplanted. Hymns have been adapted in both words and music for the use of the people. Hymns have been developed from folk melodies of the people using Scripture or simple tenets of the faith as the words and sometimes new melodies have been written in a folk style. Hymns have been created that speak to the heart, mind, and soul of the people using the musical and oral languages of the culture. All of this has happened in the past. Most of this is still happening today. Hymns, like the gospel, become a part of the culture. Music is an important way to communicate the gospel and must be done in a way that speaks to the listener in new or old patterns of song.

To understand the music of a people is to gain a better understanding of their lives, passions, and pains. This is true not only within the many cultures of the world, but also the sub-cultures of societies, i.e. the teen culture. Mission leaders have the responsibility to learn and work within a variety of musical systems so that truly new songs can be sung to God and a joyful noise can be heard in all God's world (Psalm 98).

Hymns of the Missionary

Hymns that have meaning to missionaries could be put into the following categories:

- Those that influenced their calling
- Those that sustained and nurtured them
- Those sung in the churches they attended or served
- Those that are favorites today

These categories developed from a brief survey done in 2004 with a selected group (35 in number) of active and retired missionaries and deaconesses of The United Methodist Church. They were also asked to list what they consider to be the hallmarks of a good mission hymn for today.

(One of Marjorie's retired missionary friends just happened to be included in the survey, thus she was able to get this information.)

Hymns That Influenced a Calling

Age, experience, theology, and many other things influenced the responses given by these servants of God. The hymns mentioned most often that influenced their calling to mission service were:

> "In Christ There Is No East or West"
> "O Zion, Haste"
> "We've a Story to Tell to the Nations"
> "O Jesus, I Have Promised"
> "I'll Go Where You Want Me to Go"
> "The Voice of God Is Calling"
> "Are Ye Able"
> "Jesus Calls Us"
> "I Am Thine, O Lord"
> "Have Thine Own Way, Lord"

All of the hymns listed above were identified by three or more persons as having been influential for them. Through the work of the Holy Spirit these hymns gave forth the call to service, stated the needs of the world, and demanded a response of total commitment. Two of these hymns ("O Zion, Haste" and "We've a Story to Tell to the Nations") have been looked at previously. Several others need to be examined.

John Oxenham (1852–1941), an English writer, is the author of "In Christ There Is No East or West" (#15). The hymn was part of a pageant for the 1908 exhibition of the London Missionary Society. The biblical text is Galatians 3:28. This is a hymn about the universality of faith, a faith that should not be separated by national boundaries, race, or doctrines. The third stanza of the hymn is new in *The United Methodist Hymnal* of 1989 because of the difficulty in making the language inclusive, but it does not retain the emphasis on race, as did the original. The original stanza is:

> Join hands then, brothers of the faith,
> > Whate'er your race may be;
> Who serves my Father as a son
> > Is surely kin to me.[17]

It is through service that believers are bound to Christ and to each other. The reality of this hymn is yet to be realized for there are many things that separate God's people.

"I'll Go Where You Want Me to Go" (#28) was written by Mary Brown (1856–1918). It is a gospel style commitment hymn that was sung at youth meetings and camps when the call was given for "full time Christian service." The first stanza speaks of total commitment to go wherever God sends. The second stanza expresses a willingness to speak words of love, seek the lost, and be guided in all that is said by Jesus. The last stanza echoes again the strong commitment to "be what you want me to be."

During the singing of this hymn and others like it, young people were asked to come to the altar and kneel in prayer, thus indicating their desire to answer God's call. Usually there was a pastor who prayed with them. In some settings persons were also asked to sign their name in a book as a further indication of their commitment to become a missionary, a minister, or a deaconess. In the archives of the Nebraska Conference of The United Methodist Church is still the "commitment book" of the Evangelical United Brethren Church that was used at Riverside Park, Milford, Nebraska.

In 1913 John H. Holmes (1879–1964) wrote "The Voice of God Is Calling." It is based on the call of Isaiah as found in Isaiah 6. The tune is MEIRIONYDD.

> The voice of God is calling its summons in our day;
> Isaiah heard in Zion and we now hear God say:
> "Whom shall I send to succor my people in their need?
> Whom shall I send to loosen the bonds of shame and greed?"
>
> "I hear my people crying in slum and mine and mill;
> no field or mart is silent, no city street is still.
> I see my people falling in darkness and despair.
> Whom shall I send to shatter the fetters which they bear?"
>
> We heed, O Lord, your summons, and answer: Here are we!
> Send us upon your errand, let us your servants be.

Our strength is dust and ashes, our years a passing hour;
but you can use our weakness to magnify your power.

From ease and plenty save us; from pride of place absolve;
purge us of low desire; lift us to high resolve;
take us, and make us holy; teach us your will and way.
Speak, and behold! we answer; command, and we obey![18]

In stanza one the call is given to care for the needy and for those bound by "shame and greed." The situations listed in the second stanza speak to the conditions within the United States at the beginning of the twentieth century. The third stanza states the positive response — God "can use our weakness to magnify your power." The last stanza is a prayer to be saved from pride and the good life and to be made holy for service. A promise is given to obey the call of God. John Holmes was a pastor in the Unitarian Universalist Church serving in New York City.

Hymns That Nurtured and Sustained

There were over ninety individual hymns mentioned that sustained and nurtured the missionaries and deaconesses in their work. Included in those were gospel songs, such as "He Leadeth Me: O Blessed Thought," "I Love to Tell the Story," and "What a Friend We Have in Jesus." There were songs of faith, such as "O God, Our Help in Ages Past," "A Mighty Fortress Is Our God," and "Joyful, Joyful, We Adore Thee." There were recent hymns such as "Here I Am, Lord," "Spirit Song," and "Hymn of Promise." There were also the prayer hymns such as "Breathe on Me, Breath of God" and "Spirit of God, Descend upon My Heart." The one mentioned most often is "Great Is Thy Faithfulness" written by Thomas O. Chisholm (1866–1960). Remember the refrain:

Great is thy faithfulness! Great is thy faithfulness!
Morning by morning new mercies I see;
all I have needed thy hand hath provided;
great is thy faithfulness, Lord, unto me![19]

Marion Muthiah, a missionary in Indonesia and Malaysia from 1969 to 1976, wrote:

> This hymn has recited God's goodness to me throughout my entire life and reassures me that He will continue to be faithful. It gives hope for each stage of living and helps me give thanks to God for His provision for each of my needs. I have had multitudinous blessings and I affirm God's great faithfulness to me.[20]

Dorothy R. Gilbert, a missionary from 1951 to 1991 in Congo/Zaire and Sierra Leone, told the following story about her appreciation of "A Mighty Fortress Is Our God" written and composed by Martin Luther in about 1539.

> At Oberlin College in 1939 I sang in a chorus which did Bach's Cantata based on EIN' FESTE BURG, the music that Martin Luther wrote for this hymn. At nineteen, I could only love the marvelous music without any idea of what the words would come to mean to me over the years to come. Thirty years later I had been through an evacuation from the Congo, the death of two missionaries on active duty, plus many uncertain situations of various kinds. All I can say is that when you are stopped at a road-block by a very large soldier in camouflage with a big gun and speaking a language you don't know, it is a very good thing to have this hymn running through your head.[21]

Favorite Hymns

There were as many favorite hymns as there were people who responded to the survey. Joyce Hill served in Cuba, Argentina, and Chile from 1952 to 1968 and then became a staff member of the General Board of Global Ministries. She indicated her favorite hymn is "Tenemos esperanza" (#48) written by Federico J. Pagura (b. 1923) and with music by Homero Perera. Pagura served as the Methodist bishop of Panama and Costa Rica from 1969 to 1973 and then was the bishop of Argentina from 1977 to 1989. The hymn was written during a time of war in Argentina. Joyce Hill writes of this hymn:

Pagura wrote this tango, a genre which traditionally trans-mitted hopelessness and despair and was seen as scandalous in a church setting, to transmit the hope found in the Gospel message of Jesus Christ. It is now sung throughout the Spanish-speaking world.[22]

"Tenemos esperanza" means "We have hope." The message is a powerful affirmation that because Christ is with us on the journey of life there is hope, courage, trust, and assurance in "our song of freedom for all people." The second stanza takes the stories of Jesus' ministry and death and makes his actions apply to the life of each individual. The third stanza speaks of the Resurrection and the kingdom that is to come. The last phrase uses metaphors of light, fire, and fountain in a dynamic manner. It is to this Jesus that we are to witness (Acts 1:8).

Karen Ujereh serving in Senegal indicates that her favorite hymn is "Soutiens Ma Foi." In French the words are:

> Christ est la paix recherchée de mon âme
> Ô Seigneur soutiens ma foi.
> Prends moi, Seigneur dans mon état,
> Dieu de Jacob, soutiens ma foi.

Ujereh translates this hymn:

> Christ is the peace looked for by my soul,
> O Lord increase my faith.
> Take me Lord as I am
> God of Jacob increase my faith.[23]

She says: "As I get older I am at a certain place in my life and being there I want only peace. I feel I can find it in Christ and also I feel that you never reach a point in your life where your faith cannot be increased. It can always be increased. I feel there are degrees of peace and all of the many degrees of peace can be found in Christ."[24]

Helen Sheperd is serving in Mongolia as the first United Methodist missionary in that country. She especially appreciates the hymn "When Morning Gilds the Skies" for "it lets me know there is a new day which is a gift from God. It is a day in which my life can be for the glorification of God in whatever I do."[25]

Hallmarks of a Good Mission Hymn

Many words were used to describe the hallmarks of a good mission hymn for today. Included were singable, servanthood, universality of the gospel, touch the soul, challenge. Here are a few samples:

> I think a good mission hymn should emphasize the world, the needs of the people of the world, Christ/God as a God of all persons, and the imperative for Christians to share the good news of Jesus Christ through actions and words.[26]
> — Esther Megill

> A good mission hymn should be a challenge, a call to serve. It should also be a portrayal of the need, the conditions of our world/people.[27]
> — Elizabeth J. Clarke

> A good mission hymn should speak to the head and to the heart in such a way as to elicit a response.[28]
> — Lionel Muthiah

> One of the hallmarks of a good mission hymn is to challenge our thinking about our relationship to God and to the world. Another is to use words that prick our conscience regarding the needs in the world and our responsibility as Christians to respond to those needs. A third hallmark is to directly and clearly call us to offer our lives in service.[29]
> — Betty Purkey

> The hymn should call for a personal commitment with a humble desire to share what compassion and justice can do in the world.[30]
> — Janet Galloway

> A good mission hymn should emphasize the universality of the Christian gospel and the desperate needs of God's people along with a challenge to the singer. "Here I Am, Lord" wins hands down.[31]
> — Gene Matthews

Over one-third of the survey respondents identified "Here I Am, Lord" (#34) as meeting the hallmarks of a good mission hymn for today. This hymn was written by Dan Schutte (b. 1947) in 1981 based on the call of Isaiah to serve the Lord. Schutte is a Jesuit priest and has served as director of music in several churches and college chapels. The stanzas outline what "I, the Lord" have done: creator, listener to cries, bearer of pain, tender of the poor, provider of bread. It is written in the dialogue style used by the Old Testament prophets as they told the story of God's actions and the people's denial and turning away. Then the question is asked: "Whom shall I send?" The refrain gives the response: "I will go, Lord, if you lead me."

After reading the above paper on the hymns of the missionaries, Pastor Janice called Marjorie. She was impressed with what had been learned from them, but wondered what was being sung in the churches they attended. Marjorie's response was an apology for not including that information. She had it, but had gotten interrupted and forgot. The information soon appeared in an attachment to an email sent to the pastor and Louise.

Hymns Used in the Areas Served

The missionaries reported that hymns used in the churches were primarily those that were translated into the language of the people using the original tunes. In a Palestinian church 100 percent of the hymns sung were translations, while in some churches in India only 10 percent of the hymns were translations. In Nepal it was indicated that about 40 to 50 percent of the hymns were indigenous; in Latin American countries 80 to 90 percent were translations, but more original hymns are being used in the newer hymnals. In the African countries there is a mixture of translation, folk music tunes, and new words/music, while in Korea and Japan 80 to 90 percent of the hymns are translations using the western tunes.

A favorite of Japanese Christians is "Mikotoba o kudasai" ("Send Your Word") (#68) written by Yasushige Imakoma (b. 1926) with music by Shozo Koyama (b. 1930). It was first included in the 1967 hymnal of the United Church of Christ in Japan.[32] Each stanza begins with a request that the Word be sent using the rain, wind, and dew as metaphors for the Word. This is followed by prayers for grace, power, and love in order to be ready for "your new world."

New hymnals and music resources are being developed in many countries. A supplement has been prepared for the *Hymns of Universal Praise* (remember the work done on the first edition by Bliss Wiant) by a committee of the Chinese Christian Literature Council in China with the intent of publishing in the near future a complete revised edition.

In the United States *Mil Voces Para Celebrar* was published in 1996 as the first official Spanish language hymnal for United Methodists. It contains a large amount of indigenous worship resources coming from Latin America, the Caribbean, and North America. Some of the old translated hymns have been retained and some have been retranslated. Also some hymns originally written in Spanish have been translated into English so that the faith and music of the Hispanic church can be shared.

"Te ofrecemos Padre nuestro" ("Let Us Offer to the Father") (#32) is in the new Spanish language hymnal and is part of a popular mass from Nicaragua.

> Written by Manuelito Dávila, Angel Cerpas, and Juan Mendoza in 1968, this hymn represents the community writing their theology as they experienced it through the struggles and oppression of daily living. It also represents Nicaraguan folkloric rhythms. The overall theme of the mass is that of "a people marching on." Another theme is the union of faith and daily living.[33]

Another very popular hymn is "Tú has venido a la orilla" ("Lord, when you came to the seashore") (#54). The hymn is a call to be in mission and to follow Jesus as a disciple. It is based on the story of Jesus calling Peter, Andrew, James, and John from their fishing boats and nets to "Follow me, and I will make you fish for people" (Matthew 4:18-22). The hymn was written by Cesáreo Gabaraín, a parish priest in Spain. Raquel Martínez, the editor of *Mil Voces Para Celebrar,* says:

This is a song of commitment, an invitation to follow Christ into service; it is also a song of hope, especially for those who are experiencing hardships. It is often used at funeral services, accompanied by a guitar, with Roman Catholic Hispanic constituencies. The original text is so rich that congregations are encouraged to sing it in Spanish.[34]

Korean-American United Methodists and Presbyterians joined together in 2001 to publish *Come, Let Us Worship,* a Korean-English language hymnal. The intent of this hymnal was to seek new hymns in Korean and from the worldwide Christian church; to retain some of the well-liked hymns from the early days of Christianity in Korea; to develop resources that would bridge the gap between first and second generation Korean-Americans; and to be used by the average worshipper.[35]

The Korean hymn "Jung-euh ga gang-mul chuh-rum" ("Justice Comes as River Waters Flow") (#2) was written by Hyung Sun Ryu. This hymn uses a river as a metaphor of justice and a "wildfire on the plain" as a metaphor of peace. It is through love that the jubilee of freedom can come. The second stanza speaks of the tears of suffering followed by "a new heaven and the victory." It is written in the flowing Asian style with little harmony.

Over a cup of coffee for Marjorie and of tea for Louise, they expressed amazement at all they had learned during the last several months. They were pleased with their work and ready to share it all with Pastor Janice and members of the congregation. Louise knew they had at least three sessions here for United Methodist Women. She suggested a picnic since they were enjoying such beautiful days, indicating she would contact the pastor and get back to Marjorie with the time and place. Besides, she felt the need to get away from books, papers, and the computer. At times she didn't feel as though she were retired!

---

[1] John Julian, *A Dictionary of Hymnology* (London: John Murray, Albemarle Street, 1907), 738.

[2] Ibid., 745.

[3] Ibid., 752.

[4] Ibid., 759.

[5] Tom Colvin, "Hymns out of Africa," a paper given to the Global Praise Working Group, March 1996, p. 4-8.

[6] Ibid., 2.

[7] Letter from Bliss Wiant to Frank Cartwright, staff of the Board of Missions, July 21, 1932.

[8] Chen Zemin, "Recent Developments in Congregational Singing in Mainland China," *The Hymn* Vol. 48 No. 3 (July 1997): 40.

[9] From "Selections from Hymns of Universal Praise" prepared by Bliss Wiant for use on furlough itineration in the fall/winter of 1935-36.

[10] Ibid., 3.

[11] Carlton R. Young, *Companion to The United Methodist Hymnal* (Nashville: Abingdon Press, 1993), 569-570.

[12] T. Janet Surdam, *There is Music Everywhere* (McGregor, Iowa: Self-published), 105.

[13] Delbert Rice, "Developing an Indigenous Hymnody," *Practical Anthropology* Vol. 18 No. 3 (May-June 1971): 97-113.

[14] Pablo Sosa, "Global Song and Globalization." A paper given at the Academy of Global Song, October 2003.

[15] C. Michael Hawn, "The Fiesta of the Faithful: Pablo Sosa and the Contextualization of Latin American Hymnody," *The Hymn* Vol. 50 No. 4 (October 1999): 35.

[16] C. Michael Hawn, "Sounds of Bamboo: I-to Loh and the Development of Asian Hymns," *The Hymn* Vol 49 No 2 (April 1998): 15.

[17] *The Hymnal* (Dayton, Ohio: The Board of Publication, The Evangelical United Brethren Church, 1957), 403.

[18] *The United Methodist Hymnal* (Nashville: The United Methodist Publishing House, 1989), 436.

[19] *The United Methodist Hymnal* (Nashville: The United Methodist Publishing House, 1989), 140.

[20] From personal correspondence with Marion Muthiah, November 2004.

[21] From personal correspondence with Dorothy R. Gilbert, December 2004.

[22] From personal correspondence with Joyce Hill, November 2004.

[23] French and English from personal correspondence with Karen Ujereh, December 2004.

[24] From personal correspondence with Karen Ujereh, December 2004.

[25] From personal correspondence with Helen Sheperd, November 2004.

[26] From personal correspondence with Esther Megill, November 2004.

[27] From personal correspondence with Elizabeth J. Clarke, December 2004.

[28] From personal correspondence with Lionel Muthiah, November 2004.

[29] From personal correspondence with Betty Purkey, December 2004.

[30] From personal correspondence with Janet Galloway, December 2004.

[31] From personal correspondence with Gene Matthews, December 2004.

[32] Carlton R. Young, *Companion to The United Methodist Hymnal* (Nashville: Abingdon Press, 1993), 579.

[33] Raquel Mora Martínez, "Mil Voces Para Celebrar-Himnario Metodista," *The Hymn* Vol. 49 No. 2 (April 1998): 26.

[34] Ibid., 26.

[35] *Come, Let Us Worship* (Nashville: The United Methodist Publishing House, 2001), vi.

CHAPTER 5

"Break down the wall that would divide your children, Lord."
— Olive Wise Spannaus

*I*t was a beautiful evening when Marjorie, Louise, and Pastor Janice met at the local park near the church. Each had their own picnic supper but also enough to share. After eating and watching the ducks and geese on the pond, they finally got around to their project. It had now become THE PROJECT, with all three fully involved and wondering about the next steps.

Pastor Janice made the first suggestion. She had been contemplating a series of sermons based on some of the hymns they had found as a means of getting the congregation further involved in God's mission. She was looking for the "personal response" hymn for those who could not go as missionaries, but a response that involved more than prayer and money. She knew that several of the hymns they had already identified might fit that need, but she wanted some old and new hymns to wrestle with as a congregation. Right away Louise started to name a few old hymns, but she soon realized that to do so at the moment would not be useful so she quieted down and let the conversation continue.

Marjorie got her notebook out and started to take some notes on the ideas, so that things would not get lost. She mentioned a special program called Global Praise which appeared to deal with music from around the world and thought it was something they ought to consider as a resource. Janice jumped right in on that idea and said she even had a CD and a songbook from that program of the General Board of Global Ministries. Marjorie also thought maybe some of the former "mission fields" might have developed some hymns to use in their mission work.

Louise wanted them to study the hymns related to some of the current justice issues. She was especially concerned about racism, peace, poverty, and the environment. Justice work was a part of mission and there must be some good hymns about these concerns. And then she wondered aloud: "What are current hymn writers thinking about mission hymns? Were new mission hymns being written now and what was the theology of the new hymns?"

Once again they realized their interests were becoming extensive. Some of the research could be done in actual hymnals, but some would probably need to be done on the internet. All were busy with other things, but agreed to keep each other posted. They didn't make specific assignments this time. Instead each would see what could be found on the topics and then exchange. They gave each other at least three months and then Louise agreed to pull everything together by writing "executive summaries." That phrase caused a laugh, for they all knew they would get more than a summary.

Pastor Janice, Marjorie, and Louise walked slowly to their cars, thankful for the time together and for the sense of God's Spirit in their midst. It had been a good evening!

Mission Hymns Requiring a Personal Response

For many, discerning the call and will of God is a lifelong activity. As one ages life circumstances change, one hopefully grows in the faith, and God's call also changes. What God called a young mother and father to do may not be the place of involvement that God has for persons when the children are in college. A call during retirement will certainly be different than one received at a younger age. God's call comes through the work of the Holy Spirit and each person is worthy of God's call. The Spirit works through friends, family, and through events in the world. The Spirit also speaks through prayer, Scripture, and the hymns sung in public and private worship. It is amazing how a door opens for a new response to service when it is least expected. It is also amazing how gifts and graces seem to be given for each new call.

God's call does not have to be from a burning bush as with Moses or by being struck blind as with Paul. God's call can simply be the neighbor who needs someone to sit with her child while she runs to the store; or the need for a van driver at church. In 1913, Ina Duley Ogdon (1872–1964) wrote "Brighten the Corner Where You Are"

(#51). The hymn reflects the "everydayness" of responding to God's call: by doing one's duty, by being cheerful, and by letting one's talents reflect the "Morning Star," a metaphor for Christ.

Ellen H. Gates (1835–1920) expressed similar thoughts in her hymn "Your Mission," but did so with entirely different images and metaphors. Stanza one implies that God's call is not limited to going "overseas," but is also about helping those who live within your community. The next stanza (stanza three in the original text) encourages even those without financial resources to help the needy and like Mary, study the teachings of Jesus and be knowledgeable in the faith (see Luke 10:38-42). In the last stanza (stanza six) waiting is not to be tolerated, for there is always someplace where service is needed. It is the responsibility of the Christian to find that "field of labor."

> If you cannot, on the ocean, sail among the swiftest fleet,
> Rocking on the highest billows, laughing at the storms
> you meet,
> You can stand among the sailors, anchored yet within the bay,
> You can lend a hand to help them, as they launch their
> boats away.
> ....
> If you have not gold and silver ever ready to command;
> If you cannot toward the needy reach an ever open hand;
> You can visit the afflicted, o'er the erring you can weep;
> You can be a true disciple, sitting at the Savior's feet.
> ....
> Do not, then, stand idly waiting, for some greater work to do;
> Fortune is a lazy goddess, she will never come to you.
> Go and toil in any vineyard, do not fear to do or dare,
> If you want a field of labor, you can find it anywhere.[1]

Young people were also encouraged to answer God's call in their daily lives of study, work, and play. Lanta Wilson Smith puts it simply in the second stanza of her hymn "Scatter Sunshine":

> Slightest actions often meet the sorest needs,
> For the world wants daily, little kindly deeds;
> Oh, what care and sorrow, you may help remove,
> With your songs and courage, sympathy and love.[2]

This was copyrighted in 1892 by E. O. Excell (1851–1921), a musician and music evangelist. Nothing is known about Lanta Wilson Smith.

God's call can also involve one in life-changing relationships, vocations, and avocations. As a disciple of Christ, it is one's responsibility to use the gifts and graces given by God to further God's mission. A responsible disciple also nurtures within the attitudes of love, kindness, gratitude, justice, and righteousness that can motivate an involvement in God's mission.

Olive Wise Spannaus (b. 1916) wrote in 1969 "Lord of All Nations, Grant Me Grace" (#19). The hymn is a prayer for the grace to be a true disciple of the Christ. In the first stanza there is a strong affirmation of the oneness of all God's people. In the second stanza the acknowledgment of error in word and deed is given with the hope that "the wall that would divide" can be removed. Courage is requested in the third stanza to speak out against injustice or to forgive as the oppressed victim. The last request is for a love within "my life" that can be a reflection of the love of Christ.

In "Because I Have Been Given Much," Grace Noll Crowell (1877–1969) writes of gratitude as being a motivator for mission. The hymn challenges those who have, to help those who are in need. This applies to shelter, food, and the love of God.

> Because I have been given much, I too must give;
> Because of thy great bounty, Lord, each day I live,
> I shall divide my gifts from thee
> With every brother that I see
> Who has the need of help from me.
>
> Because I have been sheltered, fed, by thy good care,
> I cannot see another's lack and I not share
> My glowing fire, my loaf of bread,
> My roof's safe shelter overhead,
> That he too may be comforted.
>
> Because love has been lavished so upon me, Lord,
> A wealth I know was not meant for me to hoard,

I shall give love to those in need,
Shall show that love by word and deed:
Thus shall my thanks be thanks indeed.[3]

Crowell was an active Methodist. She spent the first forty years of her life in Iowa and then lived in Texas. She wrote many poems, stories for children, and devotional books. In 1956 she wrote about "the global Christ," the Christ that was given to the world and about whom "all nations" were to be taught. She is concerned about the global nature of Christ, not the global nature of the church. It is with this "global Christ" that we are involved in mission.

> He (Christ) does not condemn any outpouring of love and reverence on his children's part as extravagance or wild emotionalism. He accepts every gift we make in his name as unto him. His "inasmuch" covers a wide field indeed. It covers the world. We cannot all come bearing rare perfume to our Lord, but even the smallest gift of charity is to him like incense rising heavenward. What we do for others in the world about us, he considers it as done for him, and it must ever be as a sweet smelling fragrance to his nostrils.[4]

There are several Scripture references that might be appropriate with the words above, but one certainly is Matthew 25:31-46.

At the formation of the Woman's Division of Christian Service in 1940, following the uniting of the Methodist Episcopal Church and the Methodist Episcopal Church, South, Grace Noll Crowell wrote the following poem which was read at the first annual meeting of the division on November 24, 1940.

Women and Christian Service

Today there is a challenge and a call
    To the womanhood of our new church to stand
United in one purpose. May we all
    Strive to serve our God, our homes, our land

In a higher way than we have done before;
 Let us deepen our own lives through earnest prayer;
Let us enter daily through God's open door;
 His Holy Word, and find Him waiting there.

And having learned from Him, then may we go
 As fitted able helpers of our kind
Reaching out that other hearts may know
 His power and glory...Dear Lord, help us find
New growth in grace and love that we may be
Wise in the service we would render Thee.[5]

The African-American spiritual "I'm Gonna Live So God Can Use Me" (#1) is in sharp contrast to some of the more complex hymns regarding mission. This spiritual simply states that the singer is going to live, work, pray, and sing so that he/she is available to be used by God for any purpose, anywhere, and at anytime. Such sentiments require openness to the call of God and an ability to discern what needs to be done to further God's reign of peace and justice.

Mission is about love. It is about the love of God for each of God's children. It is about the love of the neighbor and the love of self. It is about the individual's love of God. Miriam Therese Winter (b. 1938), a Medical Mission Sister, wrote this stanza from the hymn "God of My Childhood," in 1989. It indicates that mission is love in action in our world.

God of my childhood and my call,
make me a window, not a wall.
So like an icon, may I be
a sign of love's transparency,
and through the love that lives in me,
proclaim Your lasting love for all.[6]

It is this kind of love that is needed in a world divided by race, class, and religion as well as by the many differences that people tend to magnify and exploit. Fred Kaan (b. 1929) challenges everyone to set aside all differences and divisions in "Help Us Accept

Each Other" (#12). Acceptance is seen as the ability to love the other as ourselves, to care for everyone, the willingness to be changed by God, and openness to God's freeing Spirit. Although this hymn was probably written with Christian unity in mind, it also speaks of the urgency in the world to accept those of other faiths and to live together in community. Kaan is a minister of the United Reformed Church in the United Kingdom. He grew up in Holland and has served as a pastor of local churches in Wales as well as on the staff of the World Alliance of Reformed Churches in Geneva, Switzerland.[7]

Justice Issues and Contemporary Hymns

The psalmist sang about justice. The prophets called the Hebrew people to do justice and live in righteousness. Jesus preached about justice not only in his words, but also in his deeds. The church has sung songs of justice for years. Sometimes the singing has been easy, sometimes it has been hard. The intensity of the singing depends on whether justice is understood to be a requirement of discipleship and a part of God's mission in God's world. At times the singing of justice is hypocrisy and the word from Amos is needed.

> Take away from me the noise of your songs;
> I will not listen to the melody of your harps.
> But let justice roll down like waters,
> and righteousness like an everflowing
> stream. (Amos 5:23-24)

Singing becomes nothing more than noise when acts of justice, kindness, and mercy are not implemented by the congregation and the individuals who are doing the singing.

Congregational singing is part of a service of worship. The church gathers at least once a week in order to praise God, to be renewed for service, and to share in a community of the faithful. Sylvia G. Dunstan (1955–1993) was a minister in the United Church of Canada. In her hymn, "We Gather in Worship," she states several other reasons for coming together. The second stanza and refrain are:

We gather that justice may roll like the streams,
from all of our prisons, God's mercy redeems;
a home for the homeless, a strength for the weak,
good news for the poor and for all those who seek.

Refrain:
Here in hope, here in peace,
everyone has a part.
Here in faith, here in grace,
now we lift up our hearts.
God's love is a river that does not run dry;
God's faithfulness lifts like a full rising tide.[8]

This hymn can be sung to TO GOD BE THE GLORY by William H. Doane. The three images of water are powerful: justice like a stream, God's love like a river, and God's faithfulness like the tide. As Dunstan says, the church gathers to participate in God's mission.

Peace Hymns

Rae E. Whitney (b. 1927) was born in England and moved to Scottsbluff, Nebraska, after her marriage to an Episcopal priest. In "Nations Cry, Peace, Peace," Whitney refers to several passages of Scripture: Jeremiah 6:14; Matthew 5:9; John 14:27; and Romans 12:18. She also seems to be reflecting on an old Chinese proverb that traces peace in the world to peace in the nation, to peace in the home, and to peace in the heart.

Nations cry, peace, peace,
where yet there is none;
still we find conflict
with wars lost and won.
When will the whole world
decide to agree?
Such peace, said Jesus,
discover in me.

Quarrels and squabbles
tear neighbors apart;

leaders uprooted
become sick at heart;
governments falter,
lands no longer free.
True peace, said Jesus,
discover in me.

Only when people
maintain peace within
can peace and healing
of nations begin;
such understanding
the world hopes to see.
This peace, said Jesus,
discover in me.

Jesus said, my peace
I give unto you;
peace will be yours when
you love as I do.
Caring for others,
my peacemakers be.
God's peace, said Jesus,
discover in me.[9]

"Jesus Still Lives" (#65) by Suzanne Toolan (b. 1927) calls for an end to war, to the stockpiling of weapons, and to the wasting of wealth on bombs. Toolan places the thirst for power and success as a prime reason for war. The last stanza of this hymn is a restatement of the Beatitude: "Blessed are the peacemakers, for they will be called children of God" (Matthew 5:9). Toolan is a Sister of Mercy, liturgist, and writer of sacred music on the staff of Mercy Center in Burlingame, California.

In the Philippines, Christians searched for the biblical and theological grounding for their social involvement. Their study in 1985 developed into a series of workshops which speaks to the issues that Christians are confronted with today. Many of these workshops have been conducted within the United Church of Christ in the Philippines. Included in the material for one of the workshops is "Genuine and Lasting Peace." This hymn sees peace as much more than a lack of war or conflict. It maintains that peace can be lasting if, and only if, children are free, the environment is not polluted, the poor are no longer needy, and Christ is the foundation.

> Peace is the laughter of children at play
> Free from all cares of the day
> No longer victims of sickness and war
> Genuine and lasting peace.
>
> *Refrain:*
> Peace, peace, peace, lasting peace
> Peace that the world can not give
> Based on what's just, stands for the truth
> Founded on Christ our Peace.
>
> Peace is the sound of the rivers and seas
> Beauty of flowers in bloom
> Free from all human destructions and greed
> Genuine and lasting peace.
>
> Peace is the cry of the poor and oppressed
> Crying for freedom and food
> Crying for jobs and crying for land
> Genuine and lasting peace.
>
> Peace is the hope that we struggle and seek
> Until all earth's wars shall cease
> Never be cowed by the forces of death
> Genuine and lasting peace.[10]

"Help Us to Be Peace-makers" was written by Tom Colvin after the murder of Steve Biko by the South Africa apartheid regime in 1977. Colvin was in Malawi at the time leading a workshop of African church leaders from several southern African countries. Many of those in attendance lived with tyranny and understood oppression, yet knew that peacemaking was a call that could not be ignored.[11] This is a hymn that calls for justice, freedom, courage, and love. It speaks of the walls that are built "of class and race" which lead to war and fear; it contrasts worldly advice with Christ's command to love.

In the fourth stanza the concept of who is free and who is prisoner is turned around. In the last stanza the claim that freedom can only come through the cross is affirmed. The tune EVENING PRAYER can be used when this hymn is sung.

Help us, Lord, to be peace-makers,
rooted in your love and life,
bringing captives hope of freedom,
peace with justice ending strife.

All these walls of class and race
are built of pride and selfishness;
violence follows exploitation,
war erupts from fearfulness.

"Care for friends, ignore the others,"
worldly wisdom seems to say.
Loving foes and friends as neighbors
is our costly Christ-like way.

We are stronger than our captors,
free are we, but prisoners they.
Though they count us all as nothing,
love through Christ will win the day.

May we walk with you, dear Yesu,
heeding neither wound nor loss;
seeking justice for our neighbor,
finding freedom through your cross.[12]

Violence is not limited to war, abuse of the environment, brutality and rape among friends and family, or oppression of the poor. Violence can be within each person through anger, the limits placed on love, and behavior toward others. Shirley Erena Murray addresses the lack of peace within in "Gentle God, When We Are Driven" (#9). This is a prayer to turn angry words and pains around and "bring us to ourselves again" through forgiveness and "costly loving." There are no sugar-coated easy answers in this hymn, but the difficult struggles are clearly defined with very visual phrases.

Hymns Addressing Justice for Children

Children have long been the center of mission activity with schools seen as arenas for giving children not only sound education in the basics, but also education about the Christian faith. Women led the way in these missionary endeavors in the United States and around the world. They also advocated for laws against child labor, for compulsory education, and for welfare provisions especially aimed at mothers and their children. Today, women are still actively working for children on issues such as public education, children's health, and the child soldier. Mary Nelson Keithahn is a pastor in the United Church of Christ serving in South Dakota. Following the 1996 Stand for Children March in Washington, D.C., Keithahn wrote "Your Spirit, God, Moves Us to Pray" (#36). This hymn "reminds us that the spiritual gifts we receive as Christians should make us sensitive to the needs of children and willing to share God's blessings with them."[13]

In "Whose Child Is This?" (#44) difficult questions are raised about how adults deal with, and care for, children. Is it possible to care for the unknown child when the needs of a known child are not met? Are the hurts of children limited only to the physical, or are the emotional and psychological hurts just as devastating? Are children taught to hate those who are different or to love all God's children? S T Kimbrough, Jr. (b. 1936), a member of the North Alabama Conference of The United Methodist Church and the recently retired Associate General Secretary for Mission Evangelism in the General Board of Global Ministries, wrote this hymn.

Environmental Justice Hymns

"Children from Your Vast Creation" (#62) was written by David A. Robb (b. 1932) during the 1992 Rio de Janeiro Summit on the Environment. Robb is a retired United Methodist pastor and minister of music living in Georgia. He is a peace and anti-hunger advocate.[14] This hymn is a prayer for the restoration of God's creation and for a conversion from consuming, greed, and lust. The hymn is also a confession of wrongdoing which leads to war, and a hope of reconciliation with God, creation, and each other.

Fred Kaan gives a graphic description of "the state of creation" in his hymn "The Rape of the Earth." He accuses humans of being uncaring for the earth by raping the land, polluting the seas, by being excessively wasteful, and poisoning food. The last stanza is a prayer for forgiveness and a hope for purification of God's creation. This hymn can be sung to the tunes HAMBURG or WOODWORTH.

God gave us as in trust to hold
creation and its wealth untold,
but we have with uncaring hand
destroyed its green and raped the land.

We strip the trees and leave them bare,
pollute the seas, the soil, the air,
and we have never truly faced
the outcome of our ways of waste.

But now, with millions underfed
and poison in our daily bread,
we view creation with alarm;
is there still time to heal the harm?

May God forgive the curse of greed,
alert our minds to human need,
that we again may purify
the life of earth and sea and sky.[15]

In the Scriptures, a steward is seen as a servant with the responsibility to manage something that belongs to another, but at the same time a steward is a participant in whatever is happening and is affected by it. Human beings are made in the image of God with a unique responsibility to uphold God's intended purposes for creation. Humans are stewards answerable for what happens to creation and hopefully have an understanding that "the earth is the Lord's." Rae Whitney addresses stewardship in her hymn "We Are Stewards of God's Grace." She sees not only creation as a gift from God, but also God's grace and the Word. This hymn can be sung to the tune GROSSER GOTT.

We are stewards of God's grace,
called to share his gifts with others,
for throughout our human race,
all are neighbors, sisters, brothers.
>   To earth's nations, then, be friends,
>   thankful for each joy God sends.

We are stewards of God's land,
and respect, preserve, and farm it,
helping others understand
we must never waste nor harm it.
>   To all nature, then, be friends,
>   thankful for each joy God sends.

We are stewards of God's seas,
marveling at their constant motions,
and dare not the Lord displease
by the spoiling of our oceans
>   To its creatures, then, be friends,
>   thankful for each joy God sends.

We are stewards of God's skies;
faced with problems of pollution,
we seek leaders, strong and wise,
who will work for each solution.
>   To heaven's wonders, then, be friends,
>   thankful for each joy God sends.

We are stewards of God's Word,
to its witness brave and daring,
so that, when the gospel's heard,
all will seek the Christ we're sharing.
>   To all peoples, then, be friends,
>   thankful for each joy God sends.[16]

In 1994 Shirley Erena Murray wrote "I Am Your Mother" (#14). Written as a prayer given by the earth, it dramatically calls each person to remember that they are part of creation and will return to the earth as ashes and dust. The second and third stanzas suggest that the earth is to be nurtured and enjoyed, not abused or destroyed. In the last stanza the relationship of God as creator and people as caretaker is given as a challenge. The closing image "I am your mother, tears on my face" gives a sense of urgency about the state of the earth.

Hymns Dealing with Poverty

"Faith in the Service of the People" comes from the workshops mentioned above of the United Church of Christ in the Philippines. The hymn was written by Luna Dingayan, a pastor in Baguio City, Philippines. Service to the people involves the Christian in work with poor peasants, poor workers in the cities, squatters without homes, tribal peoples, women, and students. It is the church that can assist in bringing about the reign of God. The people of God are thankful for the work they do and pray for continued blessings.

> Peasants of the fields have the vision of land that is rich and free
> They till the land from dawn to setting sun, yet they remain to be poor.
>
> *Refrain:*
> Faith in the service of the people
> Faith in the service of the poor
> This is our response to the call of God
> Faith in the service of the poor.
>
> Workers of the cities have the vision of decent jobs and decent pay
> They have to work hard like the cogs of machines, yet they remain to be poor.
>
> Squatters of the cities have the vision of decent homes to stay
> They build their shanties on the sides of the streets, only to be torn down in dismay.
>
> Tribals of the mountains have the vision of land that is rich and free
> They work, struggle, and protect the land from the greed of powers-that-be.
>
> Women of the land have the vision of people with dignity
> They work, struggle, live and care for the young, and hope for a nation that is free.

Students and the young have the vision of future that's
bright and free
They work, study, learn the lessons of the past and not to
repeat history.

People of the church have the vision of Kingdom of God
on earth
A Kingdom of justice, righteousness, and peace; a Kingdom
of caring, joy, and love.

Let us come and celebrate together our joys in the service of
the poor
Giving thanks to God for all the work well done and pray
for the decade to come.[17]

Being in mission is seldom easy or comfortable. It often requires
behavioral, political, or theological changes for the participant, the
giver. One may risk rejection by friends as well as from recipients.
Most times working for justice is a long and arduous journey full of
obstacles and detours, but also containing glimpses of the new world
of God's vision. Brian Wren writes of the uncertainty and the hope in
"Spirit of Jesus." This hymn was written in 1973 following a study
tour of South Africa and can be sung to the tune CUSHMAN.

Spirit of Jesus, if I love my neighbour
out of my knowledge, leisure, power or wealth,
help me to understand the shame and anger
of helplessness that hates my power to help.

And if, when I have answered need with kindness,
my neighbour rises, wakened from despair,
keep me from flinching when the cry for justice
requires of me the changes that I fear.

If I am hugging safety or possessions,
uncurl my spirit, as your love prevails,
to join my neighbours, work for liberation,
and find my freedom at the mark of nails.[18]

Marjorie called Louise after reading this section. She was impressed with the diversity of hymns that were found, but also felt that they had only touched the surface. She reminded Louise of the hymn "Sois la Semilla" which they had discovered earlier. Marjorie suggested that the last section of the second stanza of that hymn had become very meaningful to her. She quoted:

> You are the friends that I chose for myself,
> the word that I want to proclaim.
> You are the new kingdom built on a rock
> where justice and truth always reign.[19]

"I feel that God has chosen me to do this research and study with you and Pastor Janice. We have certainly found new interpretations of the Word, and we may even help build the 'new kingdom.' And it is possible that someone may hear God's call through our activities. THE PROJECT is important!" Louise agreed.

---

[1] *The Cyberhymnal* (http://www.cyberhymnal.org).

[2] *Songs for Young People* (Methodist Book Concern, 1897), No. 4.

[3] *52 Sacred Songs You Like to Sing* (New York: G. Schirmer, Inc., 1939), 29-32.

[4] Grace Noll Crowell. *Come See a Man* (New York/Nashville: Abingdon Press, 1956), 110-111.

[5] Journal of the Annual Meeting of the Woman's Division of Christian Service, Board of Missions and Church Extension, The Methodist Church, Philadelphia, Pa. November 23-29, 1940, p. 17.

[6] Miriam Therese Winter. *Songlines* (New York: The Crossroad Publishing Company, 1996), 39.

[7] Paul Westermeyer. *With Tongues of Fire* (St. Louis: Concordia Publishing House, 1995), 94.

[8] Sylvia G. Dunstan. *In Search of Hope & Grace* (Chicago: GIA Publications, Inc., 1991), 78.

[9] Rae E. Whitney. *With Joy Our Spirits Sing* (Pittsburgh, Pa.: Selah Publishing Co., Inc., 1995), 67.

[10] *Panoramic Survey of the Bible* (Baguio City, Philippines: Institute of Religion and Culture, 1997), 39.

[11] Tom Colvin. "Songs of the World Church" submitted to Global Praise Working Group, 1999.

[12] *Global Praise 1* (New York: GBGMusik, 1996, rev. 1997), No. 29.

[13] *Sing Justice! Do Justice!* (Pittsburgh, Pa.: Selah Publishing Co., Inc., 1998), No. 4.

[14] Selah Publishing Co. (http://www.selahpub.com).

[15] Fred Kaan. *The Only Earth We Know* (Carol Stream, Ill.: Hope Publishing Co., 1999), 89.

[16] Rae E. Whitney. *With Joy Our Spirits Sing* (Pittsburgh, Pa.: Selah Publishing Co., Inc., 1995), 103.

[17] *Panoramic Survey of the Bible* (Baguio City, Philippines: Institute of Religion and Culture, 1997), 38.

[18] Brian Wren. *Piece Together Praise* (Carol Stream, Ill.: Hope Publishing Co., 1996), 124.

[19] *The United Methodist Hymnal* (Nashville: The United Methodist Publishing House, 1989), No. 583.

CHAPTER 6

"The church is meant for mission, giving glory to God's name."

— Ruth Duck

During coffee hour after church Marjorie, Louise, and Pastor Janice had a brief moment to share what was happening with THE PROJECT. All three of them were in the midst of the contemporary scene of global song with new mission hymns coming from all over the world. Louise was brushing up on her ability to play Latin rhythms, Marjorie was utilizing her linguistic skills as she tried out hymns from Russia and Cambodia, and Pastor Janice was looking at some of the theological implications of global hymns. It appeared that they were in the homestretch and they agreed to have a celebration party with lots of singing, listening, and sharing their new music and understandings. They might even have to expand the attendance pattern to include others. That decision could wait until all the research and compiling was done. The work continued with more summaries online.

Global Song

Globalization has become a key word in the last part of the twentieth century and these first years of the twenty-first century. Its meaning, purpose, and value vary with each speaker or group talking about it. Some see globalization as bringing together the world's economic opportunities—a way of allowing trade to happen among many different groups in many different countries. Others see globalization as the worldwide communication reality of global media, computers, and other technology with much work being outsourced to persons halfway around the world. Still others feel a need and a desire for the "globalization of democracy" which may lead to war, distrust, and further oppression. Globalization has positive results according to some, while others see it as having a negative and oppressive effect on people and third world nations. Globalization has made the rich much richer and the poor even poorer, but at the same time globalization has improved the living conditions within technology pockets around the world.

The globalization of the entertainment industry has created global song. One can hear songs from the United States on TV or radio in any country. There is a new category of CDs known as "World Music" available in music stores which includes music from many different countries. But are such songs really global or are they local songs that are marketed globally?

These thoughts and questions also apply to the concept of global religious music. This study has shown that the music of western Christianity was brought and "sold" to new converts in the mission fields. The motivation was not to make money but to spread the gospel, yet there was abuse and disregard of local music in the process. Today praise bands and praise music, with short and repetitious praise phrases, are a global reality and the newly exported western music. This time there is an economic impact!

The global song and its connection to the mission of the church are not about economic exploitation, theological domination, or developing a universal musical style. Instead it is about sharing the gospel as found in the hymns and songs of believers. S T Kimbrough, Jr. has put it this way:

> Since the music and songs of peoples emerge from their soil, life, and culture and provide a glimpse into their inner being, it behooves those who claim to be followers of the Creator God, who reveals the divine, creative self in Jesus Christ, to share with one another their songs. Through such sharing they express their mutual affirmation and respect of one another in creation, as followers of the same God, and they share in the innermost lives of one another; indeed, they share the rhythm, beat, and inner thought of their lives in word and music.[1]

A song does not start as a global song. A song starts in a local setting, among a certain group of people with a specific culture. "Global songs are not born global. Global songs become global when somebody else besides its authors and the people they represent, can make it his or her own. There is no global song which has not first been a local song, a song of the people."[2] A Christian song begins in the heart of a believer. It becomes a global song when other believers make it their own.

A global song is witness to what God has done and is doing in the world. A global song enables persons to strengthen community and build relationships. Global song can give reality to the biblical understanding of unity. Singing another's hymn helps each person realize anew that the faith is for all; that God's grace is inclusive. The incarnational nature of the gospel comes alive as we see the Christ in each other's songs. Using hymns from other cultures in worship challenges each person to mutual respect, mutual commitment, and mutual involvement in God's mission. A global song is a gift given in love in which we can share each other's joys and sorrows, pray for each other's concerns, and work together for justice.[3]

In 1993 the General Board of Global Ministries started the Global Praise Program. This program has brought together writers and composers, known as the Global Praise Working Group, from the worldwide ecumenical community. They share their creativity with each other and a wide audience through a series of publications and recordings. The program has provided workshops and resources in introducing and using global songs in the local congregation. The program has also taken some hymns of Charles and John Wesley and set them to new music from a variety of cultures. It encourages church musicians, pastors, and lay leaders to broaden the understanding of mission by using global songs within worship and other activities of the church. This program is about sharing the music of the people, enabling and facilitating indigenous song, and affirming each other in the faith journey.

One such song is "Brich mit den Hungrigen dein Brot" ("Break with the Hungry Your Own Bread") (#60), written by Friedrich Karl Barth (b. 1938), a German theologian and author. This hymn uses a series of phrases in a circular fashion to suggest the need for justice in the world. Each phrase is a statement of something that can be done to help someone. The hymn spells out a series of personal responses to God's call to involvement in God's mission.

Mission is described as "walking with each other in hope and joyful solidarity" in "Canção da caminhada" ("If Walking Is Our Vocation") (#33), written by Simei Monteiro (b. 1943) of Brazil. Monteiro is a United Methodist missionary serving in Geneva, Switzerland, with the World Council of Churches. She has been a professor of liturgy and music in the Methodist School of Theology in Sao Paulo, Brazil, and is a member of the Global Praise Working Group. Walking together, as this hymn indicates, gives everyone a voice, removes barriers that divide, assists in bringing in the reign of God, and proclaims the hope of a new world.

From Tanzania comes a prayer hymn to the Holy Spirit asking for guidance and nourishment for the faithful and discernment that goes beyond knowledge and liberty. "Njoo kwetu, Roho mwema" ("Gracious Spirit") (#21) is written in Swahili by Wilson Niwagila. Guidance is also requested for "our thinking and our speaking" so that the witness may always be "un-swayed by earth's allure." The term "zealous fitness" for a follower of the Christ likely refers to a wholeness that comes through Jesus and involves mind, body, and spirit working together in witness.

In the hymns cited above the original language is printed first in each song and then translations follow. This is a way of honoring another culture and its song. The Global Praise Program attempts to do this in all printed materials. They also honor another culture and its song by:

* giving full respect to musical styles;
* making sure that indigenous persons participate fully in the publication and recording projects;
* providing the best possible singable translations and para-phrases that convey the meaning of the original texts; and
* taking great care with copyright registrations.[4]

Global Praise is understood to be a mission program, one that furthers the reign of God and therefore tries to be fair and just to all involved in the songs. It is hoped that groups and individuals will attempt to sing the songs in the original language and for this reason "Romanized transliteration" is also given. Don't be afraid to try. Start with a simple song, such as the chorus of the song from Tanzania. Doing this, even though it may not be entirely correct, is another way to honor Christian brothers and sisters.

The simple prayer for peace coming from Palestine is a powerful witness to the need for peace in that part of the world. The hymn is "Yarabba ssalami" ("O, God of peace") (#61). The Arabic transliteration is not difficult and should be used with the English. Together the people of the world pray for peace in the world and in the hearts of all.

Per Harling (b. 1948) is a Swedish Lutheran pastor, a musician, and a writer of liturgy and worship materials. He is also a member of the Global Praise Working Group. In 1999, Harling was co-leader of music for an international youth conference sponsored by the Women's Division and the General Board of Global Ministries. He wrote "Nurtured by the Spirit" (#59) as the theme song for that event. The emphasis of the conference was on God's mission and the involvement of young people in that mission. This hymn is lively and works well with keyboard, guitars, and percussion instruments and can be sung as a canon. It is through the Spirit that one can walk in God's light, share and care for others, and be involved in God's mission of love. The image of seeds helps illustrate the power of God to make even the weakest able to sprout and serve.

Hugh Sherlock from Jamaica wrote "Lord, Your Church on Earth Is Seeking" (#72) with music by Joy Brown. This hymn is based on Matthew 28:18-20 and possibly other Scriptures. The first stanza emphasizes the Great Commission and the responsibility to speak and act in love. In the second stanza contrasts are made between courage and fear, light and dark, joy and sorrow, love and hatred, and peace and strife. The universal appeal of the gospel is indicated in the third stanza with the hope that "humankind may render praises to Christ."

Hymnal Development

The Global Praise Program has also helped several churches develop their own hymnals. The Russian United Methodist Church published its first hymnal *Mir Vam (Peace to You)* in 2002 under the leadership of Ludmila Garbuzova, a member of the Global Praise Working Group and a pastor in Moscow. The church in Cambodia has also developed a hymnal using a good number of hymns prepared by Sarin Sam (b. 1940), a Cambodian musician now living in Australia. Sarin Sam set biblical and Christian texts to popular Cambodian folk tunes. The hymnal was published in 2000 and contains more indigenous hymns than translated western hymns. It also has about two dozen hymns representing the global church.[5]

Similar work was done on a Lithuanian hymnal from 2004 to 2005. A French language hymnal for the French-speaking United Methodists in Europe and Africa is in process. This is mission—enabling communities of Christians to praise God in their own language and with their own music.

Ivan S. Prokhanov (1869–1935) was a hymn writer, preacher, and poet from Russia. He established the Russian Evangelical Association and published twelve books of hymns and wrote more than 1,000 hymns.[6] In "Nye khram, nye zolotoye zdanye" ("The Church of God Is Not a Temple") (#23) he writes of the humble nature of the church as being those "gathered around the cross." In the second stanza, the friends of Christ come from all over the world. The church is given grace and is renewed through the Resurrection. The last stanza is a prayer for peace from "unrest, war, grief, and strife" and an acknowledgement that life is sustained by God.

One of the hymns prepared by Sarin Sam for the Cambodian hymnal is "O mnus oeuy Preah bahn bong-hagn" ("For the Lord Has Shown to All of Us") (#25). It is a paraphrase of Micah 6:8 calling for all to "practice justice, and mercy always love, to humbly walk with God."

From Vietnam comes "Hành trang tuổi trẻ" ("We've Packed for the Journey") (#11). This is a hymn about justice involving the youth, the poor, and those who suffer. The refrain describes the bringing together of the people to worship and journey together. It is a journey of searching for the truth and "what's just." The hymn also offers to

God, "our two hands now to build a new world." This hymn and the one from Cambodia come from the people's experiences of genocide and suffering. Yet in faith they pray for justice and the rebuilding of the world.

Youth Mission Chorales

Mission is about witnessing through singing your song and someone else's song. In 1998 the Women's Division and the General Board of Global Ministries sponsored a Youth Mission Chorale to Europe and in 2001 another Youth Mission Chorale went to Asia. The purpose of each chorale was:

* to witness to the faith through song;
* to offer to young people an opportunity to see mission in another part of the world; and
* to introduce global song to the churches visited.

The European tour went to Lithuania, Latvia, Estonia, and the St. Petersburg area of Russia. The Asian tour went to Indonesia, Malaysia, Singapore, Cambodia, Hong Kong, China, and Mongolia. Each tour consisted of 20 to 25 college, university, and seminary students who spent two weeks in intense preparation to learn music in the language of each country visited and up to 15 other languages. Each young person was required to give a verbal witness at one or more concerts. They brought to the music not only their love of music, but also their love of Christ. The benefits of these tours are still being experienced in the lives of the young people. Some have become ministers; others have been involved in various types of mission work. All experienced a renewed spirituality, a sense of Christian community, and the deep love and energy God showed through the music. They witnessed to their faith not only in the music, but also as they met, traveled, and ate with the people.

Two stories need to be shared. The first comes from Haapsalu, Estonia, where the choir sang one weekday afternoon. The pastor had only been in the appointment three days, the attendance was small, and the people did not applaud because "they were in church." It did not start out as one of the better concerts, but then the Spirit came and everyone "experienced church" that afternoon. After the choir sang "Star Child" in Estonian and the pastor had thanked us profusely, the congregation could not contain themselves any longer and broke into applause. The choir ending up singing three more songs with the audience totally involved with clapping and dancing. An elderly woman came to me afterwards with tears streaming down her face and said: "I didn't understand all the words, but I do understand 'alleluia.' Thank you, for I have heard the angels singing in our church."

The other story comes from a concert in Phnom Penh, Cambodia. The day had been spent touring the city, visiting the museum where prisoners had been confined and tortured, and seeing the "killing fields," the mass graves of thousands, with the skulls visible as part of the memorial. The students had a difficult time with realities that they were too young to remember. That evening the crowd overflowed the hotel ballroom for the concert, with many young people and children in attendance. All were actively involved in the music. One of the members of the choir stood to give her witness. Her words moved everyone: "We saw today some of horrors you and your families have experienced. You being here is a strong and faithful witness to the gospel of Christ. Thank you for giving to us such a witness!"

One of the songs sung on the European tour is a prayer for guidance amidst the many changes of living. It was especially meaningful to the choir as they dealt with questions regarding faith, careers, and relationships. It was also helpful to the audiences as they considered the mission of their churches and their own involvement in God's call. "Order My Steps" was written by Glenn Burleigh, a pianist and composer from Oklahoma. Burleigh's roots are in the black church where he started serving as a pianist at the age of eleven. Today he is a teacher, a trainer of church musicians, and a performance pianist. This hymn asks God to "teach me Your will," "bridle my tongue," and "take charge of my thoughts" in order to live in this "ever changing" world. (This hymn appears on the CD accompanying this study.)[7]

Hymn Writers Speak Out

Many of the hymns looked at previously are good mission hymns for today. They are global and inclusive, they see justice as a part of God's mission, and they challenge and call for commitment. The missionaries selected what they considered to be a "good mission hymn" and gave their criteria for the hymns (see Chapter 4). It is now time to hear from the hymn writers.

Mary K. Oyer

Mary K. Oyer (b. 1923) is a professor emerita of Goshen College. She has also served on the faculty of Elkhart Theological Seminary and as an editor of *Hymnal, A Worship Book* for Churches in the Believers Church Tradition (Church of the Brethren and various Mennonite churches). Oyer studied African music for over thirty-five years. She writes:

> I have grown aware of the effects of colonialism as well as some mission activity on African churches—from the domination of Western images and music in hymns in the 60s and 70s to a gradual freedom to use idioms close to the African spirit. Those hymns of my youth that rallied Christians to send out missionaries no longer made sense. I found rather that stretching my imagination to sing a genuinely African hymn in my congregation was a far more satisfactory approach to the mission hymn.
>
> But today the question of what to sing is even more difficult for me because our government aspires to spread democracy throughout the world, using religious and specifically Christian language, thus blurring the distinction between the "kingdoms of this world" and Christ's kingdom, which is "not of this world." My teaching in Taiwan in 1999–2004 sharpened my awareness of the damage to Christianity United States power and violence is creating. Now it is even difficult to use terms I have valued, such as global hymns.[8]

When asked about the characteristics of a good mission hymn for use in the church today, Oyer wrote:

It must be one that could open our minds and ears and spirits to the varied ways in which people of other cultures perceive God's presence among them. It would ask us to enlarge our capacity for tolerance and to stretch our imaginations beyond our comfort zone. It would open the way to our experiencing the spiritual realm through the spirituality of another culture.[9]

She identifies one western hymn, "I Bind My Heart This Tide" (#4), that she can sing in the context of mission. This hymn was written by Lauchlan M. Watt in 1907. It is about the modern term "bonding," bonding that takes place with Christ, with neighbors and strangers, with God, and with peace. This is a hymn of commitment to follow Christ's teachings with all of life.

Mary Oyer ends her note by writing:

> And now an imperialistic and triumphalist view of Christianity is spreading around the world. When I think of mission in this religious climate, I find "Lord, have mercy" the most valuable text I can sing with honesty. Especially helpful are those Kyries with music from countries that we in the USA do not understand well.[10]

Three Kyries have been included (#37-39). They come from Russia, Paraguay, and Ghana. They are prayers of the people!

Pablo Sosa

Pablo Sosa has written some strong words about global song speaking to what a mission hymn should be today.

> Our global songs cannot legitimate an unjust social order. Our global songs will pray for justice, will denounce injustice, will lead us to act for justice, or they will not be truly global songs. This has to do again, with the appeal of the Psalmist (Psalm 96): "Sing to God a new song, sing to God all the Earth!" What is this new song of the earth about? What does God want to hear from us? He certainly refused to listen to the religious and political leaders of God's own chosen people when they favored oppression and injustice (Amos 5:23-24).

Should not our song be honestly, courageously and urgently telling God about the hopes and struggles of the children of God everywhere? Would God not want to listen to us sing about God's creation, and the way we are handling it? Will not our song with a clear and unmistakable sound announce the unpredictable triumph of life over death and the final feast of justice and peace for all people around the globe?[11]

A hymn that perhaps exemplifies Sosa's understanding is "Momento novo" ("In This New Moment") (#29). This hymn comes from a group within the Methodist Church of Brazil. God's call is heard in the midst of newness and the answer demands solidarity with each voice being important. Life is acknowledged to be difficult and full of fear and because of this strong ties of community are needed. It is God's gift of grace that brings people together to do God's work in love.

Brian Wren

Brian Wren would encourage Christians to sing each other's mission hymns.

While it is good to sing "our own" new hymns of global mission awareness, they should not be the main focus. For paleface congregations, singing about mission only from a white, Western perspective, however enlightened, is a kind of hymnological neocolonialism. Better by far to hear, welcome, and sing songs from our global neighbors themselves.[12]

"Here Am I" (#13) by Brian Wren is written with God/Christ being the speaker or singer. The hymn is based on Matthew 25:31-46. Christ is with and in the homeless, the children, the jobless, the pensioners, the strikers. The question is "Where are we/you? Christ is with us when we gather in his name, then why do we not live as Christ lived?"

Per Harling

Per Harling wrote "Du är helig" ("You Are Holy") (#40) as the Sanctus in a Mass for young people. Harling describes this hymn as follows:

This is a sacramental song for the Eucharist with the words rewritten from the traditional. The Eucharist is the core of the missionary Church, where people are invited to share the bread of Life at the table, singing and sharing the heavenly song to the Holy One. Being a sacramental song it is also often repeated, which is an essential part of being a missionary song. By rewriting the traditional words of the Sanctus the song seems to have become more understandable.

This song is immediately sing-able because of its easy and accessible melody. Even though the melody is in a minor key, it is full of joy. There are also two parts which makes it possible to be sung as a canon, thus making the singing fun. It is as if suddenly we join our singing with the angels, which actually is what the Sanctus is all about!

The Brazilian *samba* style is used in the song with its strong and joyful beat. Often our bodies have not been allowed to express joy together with the soul and the spirit in the sacred space. This samba beat invites the body to praise the Holy One. Such is the mission of the church; to see to the well-being of the whole human being.

The subject of the hymn is the communal "we," not the individual "I." There is a receiver of the song, a "you" to which we bring our hope and praise. To invite people to join in the communal prayer is one of the main missionary tasks of the church.[13]

God is described as holy, whole, and wholeness in this hymn. Gail Ramshaw has described the use of these words:

The author (Per Harling) has amplified the single word "holy" with the terms "whole" and wholeness," thus alerting worshipers to the linguistic connection between these ideas. We too seldom recognize "holy" and "whole" as merely two different spellings of the single idea of a unity that is unique, centered, intact, healthy. Such a gloss on "holy" widens its meaning from a more limited understanding of God's quality as being merely sinless.[14]

God is present in the here and now, especially in the wine and bread. God through Jesus the Christ is to be praised with the hallelujah of the "cosmos." This hymn has been translated into many languages and used in churches of many different cultures. It is a global mission hymn!

Shirley Erena Murray

Shirley Erena Murray, one of the best of the contemporary hymn writers, indicates that a good mission hymn for today:

> Needs clear and simple words that are the best of our everyday language in order to make Christianity relevant to people of the twenty-first century and create a reality, based on the Gospel that leads to understanding, commitment, and action. So, we need words of conviction, motivation and celebration about what we believe and want to do. We must recognize that the primary theme of "mission" is not just personal salvation but opening out, creating peace and understanding, so that justice and love can operate. This entails active work of compassion, caring for each other and our world environment, leading by example. The tunes, as in any song of conviction, motivation and celebration need to be a sense of energy, and forward momentum, matching the words. But this does not exclude less robust, more meditative hymns, which might also convey this. The music needs to be simple, access-able and with a sense of energy to complement what we are saying. This leaves open the style of music, be it contemporary or not, so long as it is catchy enough to be sung by a group of people, large and small.

> Music is absolutely essential in the church's mission. The song carries messages in a memorable, repeatable form which speech and sermons do not, music is the original "soul-food": it involves heart as well as head, music creates the dynamic for thinking/feeling/communicating at the deepest level.[15]

"Every Day" (#53) was written in 1992 by Shirley Erena Murray with music by Colin Gibson. In the first stanza a commitment to God is made to become what God intends. The second stanza acknowledges that the world is hungry and in pain and that "I can work for change" to make a better world. The last stanza calls for celebration of the Word, compassion, hope and deeds "done in your name." All of this discipleship comes about because "every day in your Spirit, I'll find the love and energy!"

I-to Loh

I-to Loh from Taiwan, a member of the Global Praise Working Group, set Shirley Erena Murray's hymn "Child of Joy and Peace" (#75) to music. Loh writes:

> When I first read this text, I could scarcely control my emotions. It made me see the reality—the general mindlessness in celebrating the Christless-Christmas. The imagery of the carol—crucifying the new born Baby on the Christmas tree—was so vivid and powerful that I could almost hear the bitter crying of the Baby on the cross. I suddenly had an urge to compose. But after many attempts, using Western scales, Taiwanese, Korean, and Indian idioms, I could not capture the mood of the text. Finally I came up with a melody in an Indonesian pelog scale—E F G B C E—letting the rhythm flow freely in irregular time to accommodate the text, and completed the song.[16]

This hymn is not the typical joyful Christmas carol. It challenges all Christians to rethink the celebration of Christmas and to truly celebrate the Christ-child as the "son of poverty." To sing this carol is to experience again the realities of the gap between the rich and poor, the hunger and hopelessness of many people, and the responsibility of Christians to share with every child. To sing this carol is also to experience the blending of words and music into a wholeness of the message.

Other New Mission Hymns

Isaiah 6:8 has been the basis for several mission hymns. "Here Am I" (#42) was written by Nolan E. Williams, Jr. (b. 1969), the assistant director of music ministries at Metropolitan Baptist Church in Washington, D.C. Williams served as the music editor of the *African American Heritage Hymnal*, published in 2001. This hymn is a contemporary black gospel hymn and emphasizes the responsibility of each Christian to "work the work and sow the seeds" and to trust God for the harvest. To be in mission is to "mend the broken hearts," "see someone distressed," and "to boldly sing."

Delores Dufner, OSB is a Benedictine Sister from St. Joseph, Minnesota. Her hymn, "The Spirit Sends Us Forth to Serve," is the theme song for the Women's Society of Christian Service of The United Methodist Church of the Philippines for 2005–2008. To be sent by the Spirit to serve requires each to work with the poor, give comfort and hope, and "to be the hands of Christ." One must also "scatter joy," "cherish life," and "serve in peace." As the women sing this hymn it is hoped they will be challenged anew to be involved in God's mission. The tune LAND OF REST may be used when singing this hymn.

> The Spirit sends us forth to serve;
>   we go in Jesus' name
> to bring glad tidings to the poor,
>   God's favor to proclaim.
>
> We go to comfort those who mourn
>   and set the burdened free;
> where hope is dim, to share a dream
>   and help the blind to see.
>
> We go to be the hands of Christ,
>   to scatter joy like seed
> and, all our days, to cherish life,
>   to do the loving deed.
>
> Then let us go to serve in peace,
>   the gospel to proclaim.
> God's Spirit has empowered us;
>   we go in Jesus' name.[17]

"As a Fire Is Meant for Burning" (#58) was written by Ruth C. Duck (b. 1947), an ordained member of the United Church of Christ. She served as a professor of worship at Garrett-Evangelical Seminary for a number of years and is the writer of many inclusive language hymns. In this hymn, mission is understood as the "reason for being" for the church. The mission is to help and serve the neighbor, "not to preach our creeds or customs." The use of the first person plural indicates that mission is the responsibility of the community. The unity of Christ's followers is emphasized in stanza three.

Contemporary events often inspire hymns. Carolyn W. Gillette (b. 1961) is a Presbyterian minister living in New Jersey. Her hymn, "God, How Can We Comprehend," was written in 1999 and can be sung to the tune ABERYSTWYTH.

> The hymn is in response to the millions of refugees who have fled their homes as the result of human-made disasters. The insane wars and social injustices that cause people to leave their homes are all too evident in our troubled world. The hymn seeks to recall the precious worth of each person. It speaks of their numerous losses as refugees and asks that we not only see their suffering, but respond to their cries for help.[18]

> God, how can we comprehend—
> Though we've seen them times before—
> Lines of people without end,
> Fleeing from some senseless war?
> They seek safety anywhere,
> Hoping for a welcome hand!
> Can we know the pain they bear?
> Can we ever understand?

> You put music in their souls;
> Now they struggle to survive,
> You gave each one gifts and goals;
> Now they flee to stay alive.
> God of outcasts, may we see
> How you value everyone,
> For each homeless refugee
> Is your daughter or your son.

Lord, your loving knows no bounds;
You have conquered death for all.
May we hear beyond our towns
To our distant neighbors' call.
Spirit, may our love increase;
May we reach to all your earth,
Till each person lives in peace;
Till your world sees each one's worth.[19]

Carolyn Gillette also wrote a hymn in 2003 about the war in Iraq and the belief of many that "war will make the terror cease." "God, Whose Love Is Always Stronger" is a challenge to let love be in charge of the world. The Scripture basis is I Corinthians 13. This is a contemporary hymn that advocates for peace.

God, whose love is always stronger
Than our weakness, pride and fear,
In your world, we pray and wonder
How to be more faithful here.
Hate too often grows inside us;
Fear rules what the nations do.
So we pray, when wars divide us:
Give us love, Lord! Make us new!

Love is patient, kind and caring,
Never arrogant or rude,
Never boastful, all things bearing;
Love rejoices in the truth.
When we're caught up in believing
War will make the terror cease,
Show us Jesus' way of living;
May our strength be in your peace.

May our faith in you be nourished;
May your churches hear your call.
May our lives be filled with courage
As we speak your love for all.
Now emboldened by your Spirit

Who has given us new birth,
Give us love, that we may share it
Till your love renews the earth![20]

The hatred, fear, and pride that are a part of war must be overcome with the courage to show love and speak peace. As a congregation sings this hymn they are praying for themselves, their country, and the world and giving each other political and peacemaking power to stand with the Prince of Peace. This hymn can be sung to BEACH SPRING.

An old hymn with contemporary music can speak anew the message of God's mission in the world. Lim Swee Hong (b. 1963) from Singapore and a member of the Global Praise Working Group, set "Ye Servants of God" (#46) by Charles Wesley to a new tune. The music is lively and challenging and with the refrain, becomes a joyful hymn of praise and commitment. Written in 1744, Charles Wesley declares that all are to proclaim the gospel and that the Kingdom is everywhere and for everyone. In the years that followed this understanding of mission did not always prevail.

Conclusion

Finally Marjorie felt that THE PROJECT was as complete as it could be. She asked Louise and Pastor Janice to join her once again to debrief around tea and coffee. They acknowledged that they were different women than when they started on their journey into mission and music. Not only did they know a lot more about mission, they also knew many different mission hymns. They had learned various theologies of mission and the songs that went with them. They were pleased that the theology of mission had moved beyond the paternalistic approach into an understanding of partnership with people and a realization that the mission was God's. They also agreed that mission hymns "reveal how alive our faith is and the dynamism of our mission."[21]

Pastor Janice shared with Marjorie and Louise some of her thoughts that she intended to use in a sermon in several weeks and a hymn she had found in Global Praise 3. She would send an email of her sermon when it was completed.

They agreed also to prepare at least two sessions for United Methodist Women around mission hymnody and perhaps do the same for the youth group. Their journey would continue as they participated in God's mission! Pastor Janice's sermon soon arrived.

God's Mission, God's Song

There is a phrase in the hymn "Sois la Semilla" ("You Are the Seed") (#31) that says "you're the waves in a turbulent sea." It causes me to think of boats going up and down in a raging ocean with high white-capped waves crashing over the boat. Neither the boat nor the people on board are in control. It is the wind that is the ultimate controlling force in this picture. To be involved in God's mission is to be like the waves powered by the Spirit of God to live, move, and act in our turbulent world.

In the early verses of Matthew 25 is the parable of the ten bridesmaids. Remember the ten were waiting for the coming of the bridegroom. Half of them waited with extra oil and the other half just waited, hoping the bridegroom would soon arrive. Ten of these women waited, but only five were prepared. Preparation is required for all who desire to participate in God's mission. It means research and study, listening and dialoguing with a variety of people about justice issues, and staying in touch with God on a daily basis. It also means standing in solidarity with peoples who are fighting for equality. It means being ready to move strategically when appropriate.

Part of our spiritual preparation is singing, and perhaps even writing, hymns that call us to claim God's promises in a manner open to the new realities of our world. Our hymns must challenge us to remember that God is in charge, that God's grace is in the world as a gift of God, that God's mission is not static and even, at times, presents us with uncomfortable prospects. The hymns we sing and write should help us wait for God's call with our lamps trimmed, before engaging further the powers and principalities of our world.

As a church, we must be imaginative in our approach to mission and our involvement in God's mission. We must be willing to imagine the newness that God intends for our world. Sarah had to imagine being a mother at an advanced age. Moses had to imagine taking the Hebrews on a long journey. Jesus told stories to help his hearers imagine a faith that was available to everyone.

The prophets wrote poetry to help the people imagine the world with God in charge. The poetry within our hymns must also articulate what the Spirit can do within our lives and the many wonders and surprises awaiting those who follow the teachings of the Christ. Jesus promised that the Spirit would always be with us as we witness in our turbulent world. Our singing should reflect our willingness to claim that promise and move ahead under the guidance of the Spirit, with boldness, as did the disciples following Pentecost. Mission calls for boldness of word, deed, and song. But remember that such boldness usually has a cost and can even be risky, dangerous, and subversive as well as redeeming. Like Peter and John, pray and sing for boldness, and then be ready for the consequences.

God's mission demands faithfulness, a sense of fidelity to God, and a trust in God that we experience through Jesus, the Christ. With faithfulness comes hope in the midst of chaos and despair. It is faithfulness that lets us believe that "God is alive in our midst in hope and joyful solidarity." It is faithfulness that lets us "sing with the sorrowful a song." It is faithfulness that "keeps us fervent in our witness." It is faithfulness that causes each "to bind myself to peace, to make strife and envy cease."[22]

To be faithful means we feed the hungry, visit the sick and the prisoner, welcome the stranger, clothe the naked. To be faithful means we "do justice, love kindness and walk humbly with our God." To be faithful means we must sing both a doxology and a lament and sometimes at the same time. To be faithful means we weep over the Jerusalems of today and celebrate each sign of God's newness in our midst. To be faithful means our song must be the song of our Christian brothers and sisters around the world.

We are "In Mission Together" (#76)! God's people will be prepared, imaginative, bold, and faithful as we serve together in mission. Let our song also be imaginative, bold, faithful, and full of God's love. Let us sing of our unity and commitment to participate in God's mission.

---

[1] S T Kimbrough, Jr., "Practical Considerations for Promoting Global Song," *The Hymn* Vol. 51 No. 4 (October 2000): 22.

[2] Pablo Sosa, "Global Song and Globalization." A paper given at the Academy of Global Song, October 2003.

[3] S T Kimbrough, Jr., "Using Global Hymnody in a Program of Global Ministries," *The Hymn* Vol. 51 No. 3 (July 2000): 7 and 8.

[4] S T Kimbrough, Jr., "Practical Considerations for Promoting Global Song," *The Hymn* Vol. 51 No. 4 (October, 2000): 25, 26.

[5] S T Kimbrough, Jr., "Using Global Hymnody in a Program of Global Ministries," *The Hymn* Vol. 51 No. 3 (July 2000): 9.

[6] *Mir Vam (Peace to You)* (Moscow: Russia United Methodist Church, 2002), xiii.

[7] Glenn Burleigh Music Workshop and Ministry, (http:www.glenmusik.com).

[8] Mary K. Oyer, personal correspondence, February 2005.

[9] Ibid.

[10] Ibid.

[11] Pablo Sosa, "Global Song and Globalization." A paper given at the Academy of Global Song, October 2003.

[12] Brian Wren, *Praying Twice* (Louisville, Ky.: Westminster John Knox Press, 2000), 288.

[13] Ibid.

[14] Gail Ramshaw, "Wording the Sanctus: A Case Study in Liturgical Language," *Worship* Vol. 77 No. 4 (July 2003): 336-337.

[15] Shirley Murray, personal correspondence, February 2005.

[16] I-to Loh, "Are All Christmas Carols Joyful?" *Global Praise 1 Program and Resource Book* (New York: General Board of Global Ministries, GBGMusik, 1997), 67-68.

[17] *Program Resource Book 2005-2008* (United Methodist Women's Society of Christian Service, Philippines).

[18] Carolyn Winfrey Gillette, *Gifts of Love* (Louisville, Ky.: Geneva Press, 2000), 79.

[19] Ibid., No. 44.

[20] Carolyn W. Gillette, *God Whose Love Is Always Stronger* (http://www.cyberhymnal.org).

[21] S T Kimbrough, Jr., *Global Praise 1 Program and Resource Book* (New York: General Board of Global Ministries, GBGMusik, 1997), 33.

[22] Hymns quoted in order given are: "If Walking Is Our Vocation"; "Break with the Hungry Your Own Bread"; "Gracious Spirit"; and "I Bind My Heart This Tide."

Hymnals and Hymnal Supplements

African American Heritage Hymnal. Chicago: GIA Publications, Inc., 2001.

Chalice Hymnal. St. Louis: Chalice Press, 1995.

The Church School Hymnal for Youth. Philadelphia: Westminster Press, 1928.

Come, Let Us Worship. Nashville: The United Methodist Publishing House, 2001. (The Korean Language Hymnal of The United Methodist Church.)

Common Praise. Norwich: Canterbury Press, 2000.

The Evangelical Church School Hymnal. Cleveland, Ohio: The Evangelical Publishing House, 1931.

The Evangelical Hymn and Tune Book. Cleveland, Ohio: Publishing House of the Evangelical Association, 1913.

The Evangelical Hymnal. Harrisburg, Pa.: The Evangelical Publishing House, 1921.

The Faith We Sing. Nashville: Abingdon Press, 2000.

The Hymnal. Dayton, Ohio: The Board of Publication, The Evangelical United Brethren Church, 1957.

Hymnal: A Worship Book. Elgin, Ill.: Brethren Press, 1992.

Hymnal of the Methodist Episcopal Church. New York: Eaton & Mains, 1878.

Hymnal of the United Evangelical Church. Harrisburg, Pa.: Publishing House of the United Evangelical Church, 1897.

Hymns Ancient and Modern. London: William Clowes and Sons, 1904.

Hymns for the Use of the Methodist Episcopal Church. New York: Carlton & Phillips, 1852.

Mennonite Youth Hymnary. Newton, Ks.: Faith & Life Press, 1956.

The Methodist Hymnal. New York: Eaton & Mains and Cincinnati: Jennings & Graham, 1905.

The Methodist Hymnal. New York: The Methodist Book Concern, 1935.

Mil Voces Para Celebrar, Himnario Metodista. Nashville: The United Methodist Publishing House, 1996.

Mir Vam (Peace to You). Moscow: Russia United Methodist Church, 2002.

The Mission Hymnal (Episcopal). Chicago: Bigelow & Main Co., 1914.

The New Century Hymnal. Cleveland, Ohio: Pilgrim Press, 1995.

The Presbyterian Hymnal: Hymns, Psalms and Spiritual Songs. Louisville, Ky.: Westminster John Knox Press, 1990.

The Sabbath Hymn and Tune Book. New York: Mason Brothers, Publishers, 1859.

Songs for Young People. Methodist Book Concern, 1897.

Sound the Bamboo, CCA Hymnal 2000. Tainan, Taiwan: Taiwan Presbyterian Church Press, 2000.

Songs of Zion. Nashville: Abingdon Press, 1981.

The United Methodist Hymnal. Nashville: The United Methodist Publishing House, 1989.

Worship in Song: A Friends Hymnal. Philadelphia: A Publication of Friends General
   Conference, 1996.

Hymnbooks and Songbooks

Africa Praise (Songbook and CD). New York: General Board of Global Ministries,
   The United Methodist Church, GBGMusik, 1998.

Bringle, Mary Louise. *Joy and Wonder, Love and Longing.* Chicago: GIA Publications,
   Inc., 2002.

Caribbean Praise (Songbook and CD). New York: General Board of Global Ministries,
   The United Methodist Church, GBGMusik, 2000.

Clarkson, Margaret. *A Singing Heart.* Carol Stream, Ill.: Hope Publishing Co., 1987.

Colvin, Tom. *Come, Let Us Walk This Road Together.* Carol Stream, Ill.: Hope Publishing
   Co., 1997.

Duck, Ruth C. *Circles of Care.* Cleveland, Ohio: The Pilgrim Press, 1998.

Dunstan, Sylvia G. *In Search of Hope & Grace.* Chicago: GIA Publications, 1991.

Fellowship Hymns. New York: Association Press, 1925.

Gillette, Carolyn Winfrey. *Gifts of Love.* Louisville, Ky.: Geneva Press, 2000.

Global Praise 1 (Songbook and CD). New York: General Board of Global Ministries,
   The United Methodist Church, GBGMusik, 1996, rev. 1997.

Global Praise 2 (Songbook and CD). New York: General Board of Global Ministries,
   The United Methodist Church, GBGMusik, 2000.

Global Praise 3 (Songbook and CD). New York: General Board of Global Ministries,
   The United Methodist Church, GBGMusik, 2004.

Good Tidings in Scripture and Spiritual Songs. Philadelphia, Pa.: Hall-Mack Co., 1931.

Gospel Hymns Nos. 1 to 6 Complete. New York: DaCapo Press, 1972.

Huber, Jane Parker. *A Singing Faith.* Philadelphia: The Westminster Press, 1987.

_____. *Singing in Celebration.* Louisville, Ky.: Westminster John Knox Press, 1996.

Hymns and Sacred Songs. Chicago: Hope Publishing Co., 1918.

Hymns of Childhood. New York: Tullar-Meredith Co., 1939.

Hymns of Praise. Chicago: Hope Publishing Co., 1922.

Hymns of Praise Number Two. Chicago: Hope Publishing Co., 1925.

Kaan, Fred. *The Only Earth We Know.* Carol Stream, Ill.: Hope Publishing Co., 1999.

Keithahn, Mary Nelson and John D. Horman. *Time Now to Gather.* Nashville:
   Abingdon Press, 1998.

_____. *Come Away With Me.* Nashville: Abingdon Press, 1998.

Lorenz, E. S. *Missionary Songs.* Dayton, Ohio: W. J. Shuey, Publisher, 1888.

Marching Songs for Young Crusaders. Chicago: Woman's Temperance Publishing
   Association, n.d.

Murray, Shirley Erena. *In Every Corner Sing.* Carol Stream, Ill.: Hope Publishing Co., 1992.

_____. *Every Day in Your Spirit.* Carol Stream, Ill.: Hope Publishing Co., 1996.

_____. *Faith Makes the Song.* Carol Stream, Ill.: Hope Publishing Co., 2003.

New Missionary Hymnal. New York: Friendship Press, n.d.

New Songs for Service. Chicago: The Rodeheaver Co., 1929.

Patterson Joy F. *Come, You People of the Promise.* Carol Stream, Ill.: Hope Publishing Co., 1994.

Pentecostal Hymns No. 5 and 6 Combined. Chicago: Hope Publishing Co., 1911.

Russian Praise (Songbook and CD). New York: General Board of Global Ministries, The United Methodist Church, GBGMusik, 1999.

52 Sacred Songs You Like to Sing. New York: G. Schirmer, Inc., 1939.

Sing Justice! Do Justice! Pittsburgh, Pa.: Selah Publishing Co., Inc., 1998.

Songs for the World, Hymns by Charles Wesley (Songbook and CD). New York: General Board of Global Ministries, The United Methodist Church, GBGMusik, 2001.

Songs of Love and Praise, Hymns by John Wesley (Songbook and CD). New York: General Board of Global Ministries, The United Methodist Church, GBGMusik, 2003.

Songs of Women (CD). New York: General Board of Global Ministries, The United Methodist Church, GBGMusik, 1998.

Student Volunteer Hymnal. New York: The Century Co., 1923.

Surdam, T. Janet. *There Is Music Everywhere.* McGregor, Iowa: Self-published.

Tenemos Esperanza, Temos Esperança, We Have Hope (Songbook and CD). New York: General Board of Global Ministries, The United Methodist Church, GBGMusik, 2002.

Wenner, Hilda E. and Elizabeth Freilicher. *Here's to the Women: 100 Songs for and about American Women.* New York: The Feminist Press at the City University of New York, 1991.

Wesley Hymnbook. London: A. Weekes & Co., 1960.

Whitney, Rae E. *With Joy Our Spirits Sing.* Pittsburgh, Pa.: Selah Publishing Co., Inc., 1995.

Winter, Miriam Therese. *Songlines.* New York: The Crossroad Publishing Co., 1996.

Worship and Service Hymnal. Chicago: Hope Publishing Co., 1962.

Wren, Brian. *Piece Together Praise.* Carol Stream, Ill.: Hope Publishing Co., 1996.

Music and Mission References

Bailey, Albert Edward. *The Gospel in Hymns.* New York: Charles Scribner's Sons, 1950.

Blumhofer, Edith L. *Her Heart Can See: The Life and Hymns of Fanny J. Crosby.* Grand Rapids, Mich.: William B. Eerdmans Publishing Co., 2005.

Bosch, David J. *Transforming Mission.* Maryknoll, N.Y.: Orbis Books, 1991.

Chenoweth, Vida and Darlene Bee. "On Ethnic Music." *Practical Anthropology* Vol. 15 No. 5 (September-October 1968).

Chinchen, Del and Palmer. "Sing Africa!" *Evangelical Missions Quarterly* Vol. 38 No. 3 (July 2002).

Corbitt, J. Nathan. *The Sound of the Harvest.* Grand Rapids, Mich.: Baker Books, 1998.

The Cyberhymnal. http://www.cyberhymnal.org.

"Developing Hymnology in New Churches." *Practical Anthropology* Vol. 9 No. 6 (November-December 1962).

Dharmaraj, Glory E. *Concepts of Mission.* New York: The Women's Division, 1999.

Eskew, Harry and Hugh T. McElrath. *Sing with Understanding.* Nashville: Church Street Press, 1995.

Friesen, Albert W. D. "A Methodology in the Development of Indigenous Hymnody." *Missiology* Vol. X No. 1 (January 1982).

Global Praise 1 Program and Resource Book. New York: General Board of Global Ministries, The United Methodist Church, GBGMusik, 1997.

Grace Upon Grace. The Mission Statement of The United Methodist Church. Nashville: Graded Press, 1990.

Hardesty, Nancy A. *Women Called to Witness.* Knoxville: The University of Tennessee Press, 1999.

Hawn, C. Michael. "Sounds of Bamboo: I-to Loh and the Development of Asian Hymns." *The Hymn* Vol. 49 No. 2 (April 1998).

_____. "The Fiesta of the Faithful: Pablo Sosa and the Contextualization of Latin American Hymnody." *The Hymn* Vol. 50 No. 4 (October 1999).

Hobbs, June Hadden. *"I Sing for I Cannot Be Silent."* Pittsburgh: University of Pittsburgh Press, 1997.

Hustad, Donald P. *Jubilate! Church Music in the Evangelical Tradition.* Carol Stream, Ill.: Hope Publishing Co., 1981.

Julian, John, editor. *A Dictionary of Hymnology.* London: John Murray, Albemarle Street, 1907.

Kimbrough, S T, Jr. *Music and Mission: Foundations of Theology and Practice of Global Song.* New York: General Board of Global Ministries, The United Methodist Church, GBGMusik, 2006.

Kimbrough, S T, Jr. "Using Global Hymnody in a Program of Global Ministries." *The Hymn* Vol. 51 No. 3 (July 2000).

_____. "Practical Considerations for Promoting Global Song." *The Hymn* Vol. 51 No. 4 (October 2000).

King, Roberta. "Toward a Discipline of Christian Ethnomusicology: A Missiological Paradigm." *Missiology* Vol. XXXII No. 3 (July 2004).

McCutchan, Robert Guy. *Our Hymnody.* Nashville: Abingdon Press, 1937.

Messer, Donald E. *A Conspiracy of Goodness.* Nashville: Abingdon Press, 1992.

Morse, R. LaVerne. "Ethnomusicology: A New Frontier." *Evangelical Missions Quarterly* Vol. 11 No. 1 (January 1975).

Mouw, Richard J. and Mark A. Noll, editors. *Wonderful Words of Life.* Grand Rapids, Mich.: William B. Eerdmans Publishing Co., 2004.

Nelson, David. "Crossing the Music Threshold." *Evangelical Missions Quarterly* (April 1999).

Newbigin, Lesslie. *Mission In Christ's Way.* New York: Friendship Press, 1987.

Osbeck, Kenneth W. *Amazing Grace.* Grand Rapids, Mich.: Kregel Publications, 2002.

Rice, Delbert. "Developing An Indigenous Hymnody." *Practical Anthropology* Vol. 18 No. 3 (May-June 1971).

Robert, Dana L. *American Women in Mission.* Macon, Ga.: Mercer University Press, 1997.

Ryden, E. E. *Christian Hymnody.* Rock Island, Ill.: Augustana Press, 1959.

Schilling, S. Paul. *The Faith We Sing.* Philadelphia: Westminster Press, 1983.

Schmidt, Jean Miller. *Grace Sufficient: A History of Women in American Methodism 1760-1939.* Nashville: Abingdon Press, 1999.

Shawyer, Richard. "Indigenous Worship." *Evangelical Missions Quarterly* Vol. 38 No. 3 (July 2002).

Sizer, Sandra S. *Gospel Hymns and Social Religion.* Philadelphia: Temple University Press, 1978.

Smith, Nicholas. *Songs From the Hearts of Women.* Cambridge: University Press, 1903.

Sohl, Joyce D. *A Journey in Song.* New York: Women's Division, General Board of Global Ministries, The United Methodist Church, 1999.

_____. *Sing the Wondrous Love of Jesus.* New York: General Board of Global Ministries, The United Methodist Church, GBGMusik, 2006.

Stanley, Susie C. *Holy Boldness.* Knoxville: University of Tennessee Press, 2002.

Tamke, Susan S. *Make a Joyful Noise Unto the Lord.* Athens, Ohio: Ohio University Press, 1978.

Verkuyl, J., translated and edited by Dale Cooper. *Contemporary Missiology.* Grand Rapids, Mich.: William B. Eerdmans Publishing Co., 1978.

Warren, James I., Jr. *O For a Thousand Tongues.* Grand Rapids, Mich.: Francis Asbury Press, 1988.

Westermeyer, Paul. *With Tongues of Fire.* St Louis, Mo.: Concordia Publishing House, 1995.

_____. *Let Justice Sing Hymnody and Justice.* Collegeville, Minn.: The Liturgical Press, 1998.

Whaling, Frank, editor. *John and Charles Wesley.* Mahwah, N.J.: Paulist Press, 1981.

Wiant, Allen Artz. *A New Song for China. A Biography of Bliss Mitchell Wiant.* Victoria, Canada: Trafford Publishing, 2003.

"Women and Mission." *International Review of Mission* Vol. 95 No. 368 (January 2004).

"Women in Mission." *International Review of Mission* Vol. LXXXI, No. 322 (April 1992).

Wren, Brian. *Praying Twice.* Louisville, Ky.: Westminster John Knox Press, 2000.

Young, Carlton R. *Companion to The United Methodist Hymnal.* Nashville: Abingdon Press, 1993.

I'm gonna live so God can use me   1

African American spiritual

African American spiritual
arr., Wendell Whalum

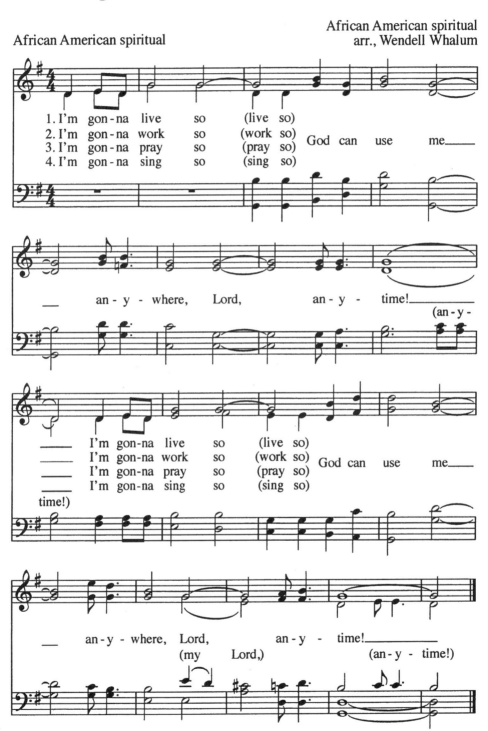

1. I'm gon-na live so (live so) God can use me
2. I'm gon-na work so (work so)
3. I'm gon-na pray so (pray so)
4. I'm gon-na sing so (sing so)

an-y-where, Lord, an-y-time! (an-y-

I'm gon-na live so (live so) God can use me
I'm gon-na work so (work so)
I'm gon-na pray so (pray so)
I'm gon-na sing so (sing so)

time!)

an-y-where, Lord, an-y-time!
(my Lord,) (an-y-time!)

2 Justice comes as river waters flow

Jung-euh ga gang-mul chuh-rum

words and music, Hyung Sun Ryu
Korean translit., Soonae Kang, 2006
English trans., Edward Poitras

Korean translit.:
1. Jung-euh ga gang - mul chuh - rum, pyung - hwa ga
2. Noon-mul gwa see rul boo - ree - myeo, jee - nah - ohn

English:
1. Jus - tice comes as riv - er wa - ters flow, peace spreads forth like
2. When we sowed 'twas a day for tears, now the time of

deul - bool chuh - rum, sah - rang yi hat - bit chuh-
soo - nan eh se - wol, bo - ah - rah woo - ree noon ah -
wild - fire on the plain, love shines forth like sun - shine af - ter
suf - fer - ing has passed, and be - fore our long - ing eyes

rum, ha - nah - nim joo - shin seng - myung bo - deum - uh,
peh sae ha - neul yi whal - zak yeo - lin - da.
rain, em - brac - ing all the life God has made.
we see a new heav - en and the vic - to - ry.

Refrain

Hee - nyon eul hyang - hae hahm - keh gah - neun gil, joo
We march on the road to the ju - bi - lee, the

eh yak - sok gut - geh mee - deu - myeo, ill - gob - bun sick ill -
Lord's prom - ise lead - ing us to - day, tho' we fail and fall

gob - bun num - uh - juh - doh, yak - sok eul gut - geh mee - deu - myeo.
sev - en times on our way, we trust God to set us all free.

We all are one in mission

3

Rusty Edwards, 1986

Memmingen ms., 17 century
harm., George R. Woodward, 1904

1. We all are one in mis - sion, we all are one in call, our var - ied gifts u - nit - ed by Christ, the Lord of all. A sin - gle, great com - mis - sion com - pels us from a - bove to plan and work to - geth - er that all may know Christ's love.

2. We all are called for ser - vice to wit - ness in God's name; our min - is - tries are dif - f'rent our pur - pose is the same: to touch the lives of oth - ers by God's sur - pris - ing grace so ev - ery folk and na - tion may feel God's warm em - brace.

3. Now let us be u - nit - ed and let our song be heard. Now let us be a ves - sel for God's re - deem - ing word. We all are one in mis - sion, we all are one in call, our var - ied gifts u - nit - ed by Christ, the Lord of all.

4   I bind my heart this tide

Lauchlan M. Watt,
The Tryst, A Book of the Soul, 1907   J. Randall Zercher, 1965

1. I bind my heart this tide to the
2. I bind my soul this day to the
3. I bind my heart in thrall to the
4. I bind my-self to peace, to make

Gal - i - le - an's side, to the wounds of
neigh - bor far a - way, and the stran - ger
God, the Lord of all, to the God, the
strife and en - vy cease. God, knit thou

Cal - va - ry, to the Christ who died for me.
near at hand, in this town, and in this land.
poor one's friend, and the Christ whom he did send.
sure the cord of my thrall - dom to my Lord!

Jesus Christ sets free to serve 5

words and music, I-to Loh, 1985

Introduction, measures 3 and 4

Changgo drum

Je - sus Christ sets free to serve all of hu - man-
kind in love; we are part- ners in God's mis-sion,
strug-gling for the full - ness of life. Lord, our Mas - ter,
help us care, share our gifts, our bur - dens bear.

6   Christ for the world we sing

Samuel Wolcott, 1869   Felice de Giardini, 1769

1. Christ for the world we sing, the world to
2. Christ for the world we sing, the world to
3. Christ for the world we sing, the world to
4. Christ for the world we sing, the world to

Christ we bring, with lov - ing zeal;
Christ we bring, with fer - vent prayer;
Christ we bring, with one ac - cord;
Christ we bring, with joy - ful song;

the poor, and them that mourn, the faint and o - ver - borne,
the way - ward and the lost, by rest - less pas - sions tossed,
with us the work to share, with us re - proach to dare,
the new - born souls, whose days, re - claimed from er - ror's ways,

sin - sick and sor - row - worn, whom Christ doth heal.
re - deemed at count - less cost, from dark de - spair.
with us the cross to bear, for Christ our Lord.
in - spired with hope and praise, to Christ be - long.

Come! Peace of God

May Rowland, 1935

Lily Rendle, 1935

1. Come! Peace of God, and dwell a - gain on earth,
2. Break ev - ery wea - pon forged in fires of hate,
3. Bring self - ish lives from shad - ow - lands of loss
4. Come! Bless - ed Peace, as when, in hush of eve,

come, with the calm that hailed thy Prin - ce's birth,
turn back the foes that would as - sail thy gate;
in - to the ra - diance of the Sav - ior's cross,
God's ben - e - dic - tion falls on souls who grieve;

come, with the heal - ing of thy gen - tle touch,
where fields of strife lie des - o - late and bare
where, in that gift— so pre - cious, yet so lone—
as shines a star when wea - ry day de - parts,

come, Peace of God, that this world needs so much.
take thy sweet flow'rs of peace and plant them there.
life finds its broth - er - hood and love its throne.
come! Peace of God, and rule with - in our hearts.

8 From Greenland's icy mountains

Reginald Heber, 1819

Lowell Mason, 1823

1. From Green-land's i - cy moun - tains, from In - dia's cor - al
2. What though the spi - cy breez - es blow soft o'er Cey - lon's
3. Can we, whose souls are light - ed with wis-dom from on
4. Waft, waft, ye winds, his sto - ry, and you, ye wa - ters,

strand, where Af-ric's sun - ny foun - tains roll down their gold-en
isle; though ev -'ry pros-pect pleas - es, and on - ly man is
high, can we to men be-night - ed the lamp of life de-
roll, till, like a sea of glo - ry, it spreads from pole to

sand; from many an an - cient riv - er, from many a palm - y
vile: in vain with lav - ish kind - ness the gifts of God are
ny? Sal - va - tion! O sal - va - tion! The joy - ful sound pro-
pole; till o'er our ran-somed na - ture the Lamb for sin - ners

plain, they call us to de - liv - er their land from er - ror's chain.
strown; the hea-then in his blind - ness bows down to wood and stone.
claim, till each re-mot - est na - tion has learn'd Mes- si - ah's name.
slain, Re-deem-er, King, Cre - a - tor, in bliss re-turns to reign.

Gentle God, when we are driven 9

Shirley Erena Murray, 1992   Jillian Bray, 1992

1. Gen - tle God, when we are driv - en past the lim - its of our love, when our hurt would have a weap - on and the hawk de - stroy the dove, at the cost of seem - ing weak, help us turn the oth - er cheek.

2. Gen - tle Spir - it, when our rea - son clouds in an - ger, twists in fear, when we strike in - stead of strok - ing, when we bruise and sting and smear, cool our burn - ing, take our pain, bring us to our - selves a - gain.

3. In the mir - ror of earth's mad - ness let us see our rav - aged face, in the tur - moil of all peo - ple let com - pas - sion find a place, touch our heart to make a - mends, see our en - e - mies as friends.

4. Let our strength be in for - giv - ing as for - giv - en we must be, one to one in cost - ly lov - ing, find - ing trust and grow - ing free, gen - tle God, be our re - lease, gen - tle Spir - it, teach us peace.

10 Go, make of all disciples

Leon M. Adkins, 1955

Henry T. Smart, 1835

1. "Go, make of all dis-ci-ples." We hear the call, O Lord, that comes from thee, our Fa-ther, in thy e-ter-nal Word. In-spire our ways of learn-ing through ear-nest, fer-vent prayer, and let our dai-ly liv-ing re-veal thee ev-ery-where.

2. "Go, make of all dis-ci-ples," bap-tiz-ing in the name of Fa-ther, Son, and Spir-it, from age to age the same. We call each new dis-ci-ple to fol-low thee, O Lord, re-deem-ing soul and bod-y by wa-ter and the Word.

3. "Go, make of all dis-ci-ples." We at thy feet would stay un-til each life's vo-ca-tion ac-cents thy ho-ly way. We cul-ti-vate the na-ture God plants in ev-ery heart, re-veal-ing in our wit-ness the mas-ter teach-er's art.

4. "Go, make of all dis-ci-ples." We wel-come thy com-mand. "Lo, I am with you al-ways." We take thy guid-ing hand. The task looms large be-fore us; we fol-low with-out fear; in heaven and earth thy pow-er shall bring God's king-dom here.

We've packed for the journey   **11**

English para., S T Kimbrough, Jr.
based on a trans. from Vietnamese by Phu Xuan Ho   trad. Vietnamese melody

Refrain

We come from four cor-ners of the earth. O
Lord, from all vil-lag-es we come, pil-grims jour-ney-ing
forth to be in the house of God, in the house of God. *Fine*

1. We've packed for the jour - ney the pride of our
2. We've packed for the jour - ney the suf - f'ring of
3. We've packed for the jour - ney our life's bit - ter
4. We've packed for the jour - ney the search for the

youth; we've packed for the jour - ney our des - ti - ny's
all; we've packed for the jour - ney the lot of the
taste; we've packed for the jour - ney the an - guish of the
truth; we've packed for the jour - ney the search for what's

pain.
poor.   We of - fer to God, Spir - it Guide,___
earth.
just.

D.C. al Fine

___ our two hands now to build a new world.

12 Help us accept each other

Fred Kaan, 1974

John Ness Beck, 1977

1. Help us ac-cept each oth-er as Christ ac-cept-ed us;
2. Teach us, O Lord, your les-sons, as in our dai-ly life
3. Let your ac-cep-tance change us, so that we may be moved
4. Lord, for to-day's en-coun-ters with all who are in need,

teach us as sis-ter, broth-er, each per-son to em-brace.
we strug-gle to be hu-man and search for hope and faith.
in liv-ing sit-u-a-tions to do the truth in love;
who hun-ger for ac-cep-tance, for righ-teous-ness and bread,

Be pres-ent, Lord, a-mong us, and bring us to be-lieve
Teach us to care for peo-ple, for all, not just for some,
to prac-tice your ac-cep-tance, un-til we know by heart
we need new eyes for see-ing, new hands for hold-ing on;

we are our-selves ac-cept-ed and meant to love and live.
to love them as we find them, or as they may be-come.
the ta-ble of for-give-ness and laugh-ter's heal-ing art.
re-new us with your Spir-it; Lord, free us, make us one!

Here am I

13

Brian Wren, 1983

Daniel Charles Damon, 1995

1. Here am I, where un-der-neath the brid-ges
2. Here am I, with peo-ple in the line-up,
3. Here am I, where two or three are gath-ered,

in our win-ter cit-ies home-less peo-ple sleep.
anx-ious for a hand-out, ach-ing for a job.
read-y to be al-tered, shar-ing wine and bread.

Here am I, where in de-cay-ing hous-es lit-tle chil-dren
Here am I, when pen-sion-ers and strik-ers sing and march to-
Here am I, where those who hear the preach-ing change their way of

shiv-er, cry-ing at the cold. Where are you?
geth-er, want-ing some-thing new. Where are you?
liv-ing, find the way to life. Where are you?

14 I am your mother
Earth Prayer

Shirley Erena Murray, 1996

Per Harling, 1996
harm., Carlton R. Young

1. I am your moth-er: do not neg-lect me! Child-ren pro-tect me— I need your trust; my breath is your breath, my death is your death, ash-es to ash-es, dust in-to dust.

2. I am your nur-ture: do not de-stroy me! Love and en-joy me, sa-vor my fruit; my good is your good, my food is your food, wa-ter and flow-er, branch-es and root.

3. I am your lodg-ing: do not a-buse me! ten-der-ly use me, sooth-ing my scars; my health is your health, my wealth is your wealth, shin-ing with prom-ise, set a-mong stars.

4. God is our mak-er: do not de-ny God, chal-lenge, de-fy God, threat-en this place; life is to cher-ish,— care, or we per-ish! I am your moth-er,— tears on my face.

In Christ there is no east or west 15

sts. 1, 2, 4, John Oxenham, 1913
st. 3, Laurence Hull Stookey, 1987

African American spiritual
adapt. and arr., Harry T. Burleigh, 1939

1. In Christ there is no east or west, in
2. In Christ shall true hearts ev - ery - where their
3. In Christ is neith - er Jew nor Greek, and
4. In Christ now meet both east and west, in

him no south or north; but one great fel - low -
high com - mun - ion find; his ser - vice is the
neith - er slave nor free; both male and fe - male
him meet south and north; all Christ - ly souls are

ship of love through - out the whole wide earth.
gold - en cord close bind - ing hu - man - kind.
heirs are made, and all are kin to me.
one in him through - out the whole wide earth.

16 Jesu, Jesu

Tom Colvin, 1969

Ghanaian folk song; adapt., Tom Colvin, 1969
harm., Charles H. Webb, 1988

Refrain

Je - su, Je - su, fill us with your love, show
us how to serve the neigh-bors we have from you. *Fine*

1. Kneels at the feet of his friends, si - lent - ly wash - es their
2. Neigh - bors are rich and poor, neigh - bors are black and
3. These are the ones we should serve, these are the ones we should
4. Lov - ing puts us on our knees, serv - ing as though we are
5. Kneel at the feet of our friends, si - lent - ly wash - ing their

D. C. al Fine

feet, Mas - ter who acts as a slave to them.
white, neigh - bors are near and far a - way.
love; all these are neigh-bors to us and you.
slaves, this is the way we should live with you.
feet, this is the way we should live with you.

Jesus belongs to all children 17

Alice Jean Cleator, 1934 — Arthur Grantle, 1934

1. Je - sus be - longs to all chil-dren, not just to this coun - try of
2. Je - sus be - longs to all chil-dren, to yel - low and brown, black and
3. Je - sus be - longs to all chil-dren, let's send the glad ti - dings a -

ours, but to those far a - way, at work or at play, in
white, the Son of God's love sent down from a - bove, he
way. Let's give all we can to aid in the plan that

Refrain

coun-tries of snow and of flow'rs.
came that they all might have light.
all may know Je - sus to - day.

Je-sus be-longs to all chil - dren, in

cot-tage or grand pal - ace hall. This mes-sage so true send

all the world through that Je - sus be - longs to us all!

18 Jesus shall reign

Isaac Watts, 1719

John Hatton, 1793

1. Je - sus shall reign wher - e'er the sun
2. To Je - sus end - less prayer be made,
3. Peo - ple and realms of ev - ery tongue
4. Bless - ings a - bound wher - e'er he reigns;
5. Let ev - ery crea - ture rise and bring

does it suc - ces - sive jour - neys run;
and end - less prais - es crown his head;
dwell on his love with sweet - est song;
all pris - oners leap and loose their chains;
hon - ors pe - cu - liar to our King;

his king - dom spread from shore to shore,
his name like sweet per - fume shall rise
and in - fant voic - es shall pro - claim
the wea - ry find e - ter - nal rest,
an - gels de - scend with songs a - gain,

till moons shall wax and wane no more.
with ev - ery morn - ing sac - ri - fice.
their ear - ly bless - ings on his name.
and all who suf - fer want are blest.
and earth re - peat the loud a - men!

Lord of all nations

19

Olive Wise Spannaus, 1969

Martin Luther, 1543

1. Lord of all na - tions, grant me grace
2. For - give me, Lord, where I have erred
3. Give me your cour - age, Lord, to speak
4. With your own love may I be filled

to love all peo - ple, ev - ery race,
by love - less act and thought - less word.
when - ev - er strong op - press the weak.
and by your Ho - ly Spir - it willed,

to see each mor - tal as I ought,
Break down the wall that would di - vide
Should I my - self as vic - tim live,
that all whose lives are touched by mine,

my kin - dred, whom your love has bought.
your chil - dren, Lord, on ev - 'ry side.
re - mem - b'ring you, may I for - give.
may know your heal - ing touch di - vine.

20   Lord, speak to me

Frances R. Havergal, 1872   adapt. from Robert Schumann, 1839

1. Lord, speak to me, that I may speak in
2. O strength - en me, that while I stand firm
3. O teach me, Lord, that I may teach the
4. O fill me with thy full - ness, Lord, un -
5. O use me, Lord, use ev - en me, just

liv - ing ech - oes of thy tone; as thou hast sought, so
on the rock, and strong in thee, I may stretch out a
pre - cious things thou dost im - part; and wing my words, that
til my ver - y heart o'er - flow in kin - dling thought and
as thou wilt, and when, and where, un - til thy bless - ed

let me seek thine err - ing chil - dren lost and lone.
lov - ing hand to wres - tlers with the trou - bled sea.
they may reach the hid - den depths of many a heart.
glow - ing word, thy love to tell, thy praise to show.
face I see, thy rest, thy joy, thy glo - ry share.

Njoo kwetu, Roho mwema　21
Gracious Spirit

Ganda Melody
harm., C. Michael Hawn

Wilson Niwagila

Swahili:
1. Njo - o kwe - tu, Ro - ho mwe - ma, M - fa - ri - ji wa -
2. Ut - fa - ny - e wa - a - mi - ni wa Ye - su Mwo - ko -
3. Kwa hu - ru - ma tu - ba - ri - ki, tu - i - shi na we -
4. Ro - ho mwe - ma M - fa - ri - ji, u - tu - pe he - ki -
5. Tu - du - mi - she tu - we ha - i na u - kwe - li wa -

tu. Tu - fu - ndi - she ya mbi - ngu - ni,
zi. Tu - ka - i - shi ki - ku - ndi - ni,
we. Tu - ka - te - nde ki - la ki - tu
ma; Tu - ki - wa - za na ku - te - nda,
ko. Tu - si - vu - twe na du - ni - a,

Refrain

tu - we wa - tu wa - pya.
ka - ni - sa - ni mwa - ko.
ku - o - ngo - zwa na - we. Njo - o,
yo - te ya - we ya - ko.
tu - shu' - die ne - e - ma.

njo - o, njo - o, Ro - ho mwe - ma.

22 Gracious Spirit
Njoo kwetu, Roho mwema

Wilson Niwagila
trans., Howard S. Olson

Ganda Melody
harm., C. Michael Hawn

1. Gra - cious Spir - it, heed our plead - ing, fash - ion us all a - new. It's your lead - ing that we're need - ing, help us to fol - low you.
2. Come to teach us, come to nour - ish those who be - lieve in Christ. Bless the faith - ful, may they flour - ish, strength - ened by grace un - priced.
3. Guide our think - ing and our speak - ing done in your ho - ly name. Mo - ti - vate all in their seek - ing, free - ing from guilt and shame.
4. Not mere knowl - edge, but dis - cern - ment, nor root - less lib - er - ty; turn dis - qui - et to con - tent - ment, doubt in - to cer - tain - ty.
5. Keep us fer - vent in our wit - ness; un - swayed by earth's al - lure. Ev - er grant us zeal - ous fit - ness, which you a - lone as - sure.

Refrain

Come, come, come, Ho - ly Spir - it, come.
Swahili: Njo - o, njo - o, njo - o, Ro - ho mwe - ma.

Nye khram, nye zolotoye zdanye 23
The church of God is not a temple

Ivan S. Prokhanov

trad. Russian melody

Russian translit.:

1. Nye khram, nye zo - lo - to - ye zdan - ye, Nye krug a - to - bran- nykh dru - zey, Khris - tom is - kup - len - nykh lu - dei.
2. Sah - bran - ye dush s pus - ty - ni yu - ga, Aht za - pad - nykh, vos - toch - nykh stran, Aht stra - shen snyezh - ny u - ra - gan.
3. Khris - to - va Tzer - kov mir vos - kryes - shi Ee ahb - nov - len - ny rod lud - skoi. Ye - yo nya - dye - lit crest Pah - nyes - shi Ee Ee no - vym nye - bom, ee zem - lyoi.
4. Nye dlya pah - ko - ya v mi - re e - tom Khris - to - va Tzer - kov is - bra - na, Zdyes Bo - gom ee yE - you za - nye - tol - ko beet - va suzh - dye - na.

krug a - to - bran- nykh dru - zey, Khris -
za - pad - nykh, vos - toch - nykh stran, Aht
ahb - nov - len - ny rod lud - skoi. Ye -
to - va Tzer - kov is - bra - na, Zdyes

to - va tzer - kov yest sah - bra - nye Kres -
se - ve - ra, gde vyech - na vyu - ga, Ee
yo nya - dye - lit crest Pah - nyes - shi Ee
Bo - gom ee yE - you za - nye - tom yEi

tom is - kup - len - nykh lu - dei.
stra - shen snyezh - ny u - ra - gan.
no - vym nye - bom, ee zem - lyoi.
tol - ko beet - va suzh - dye - na.

24 The church of God is not a temple
Nye khram, nye zolotoye zdanye

Ivan S. Prokhanov
English trans., S T Kimbrough, Jr.

trad. Russian melody

1. The church of God is not a tem - ple one
   must with fin - est gold em - boss, nor
   the e - lect as the ex - am - ple, but
   peo - ple gath - ered 'round the cross.

2. It gath - ers souls from dis - tant pla - ces, from
   south - ern climes, from East and West, from
   north - ern moun - tains' snow - capped tra - ces— each
   one's a friend, and not a guest.

3. The church of Christ is re - sur - rect - ed from
   death to life with grace im - bued. Christ,
   once up - on the cross re - ject - ed, all
   earth and heaven has now re - newed.

4. For peace the church is ev - er yearn - ing a -
   mid un - rest, war, grief, and strife. God's
   peace - born church is al - ways learn - ing: through
   strug - gle God sus - tains its life.

O mnus oeuy Preah bahn bong-hagn 25
For the Lord has shown to all of us

Micah 6:8 para. and music, Sarin Sam
English para., S T Kimbrough, Jr.

Khmer translit.: O mnus oeuy Preah bahn bong-hagn neak heuy oy skorl sek-kdey del

English: For the Lord has shown to all of us and told us what is

loar teh Preah Am-Chas oy neak twer douch-mdeck nor keur

good; and what does God re-quire of us: to

oy pror-pret tair loar tahm plow soch-reth yutek-tor heuy

prac-tice jus - tice, and mer-cy al-ways love, to

sror-lagn kdey sobo-bros. Trov deur chear muy ning Preah ney

hum-bly walk with God, to prac - tice jus-tice, to love

kluon oy batin chorb snith morm moon doy kdey so-pheap reap teap.

mer - cy, and to walk hum-bly, hum-bly with our God.

26 War's madness and confusion
Peace through his cross

Catherine Baker, 1945   Samuel S. Wesley, 1864

1. War's mad-ness and con-fu-sion on land and o-cean cease, for
2. His cross— the sym-bol calls us to con-tem-plate its prayer, to
3. Comes peace, world un-der-stand-ing, su-prem-a-cy of good— all

at this ve-ry mo-ment Christ works en-dur-ing peace. In-
speak with cheer and wis-dom, to give the need-y care; to
peo-ples, class-es, ra-ces, be-liefs, a broth-er-hood. Greed,

spite of black-ened land-scape, the waste, the grief, the loss, the
bring the means of heal-ing where sick in an-guish toss, to
sel-fish-ness and hat-red melt as un-want-ed dross— through

count-less homes made lone-ly— love sig-nals from the cross.
help eyes tor-ture-blind-ed be-hold the light-ed cross.
rec-on-cil-ing pow-er peace comes, peace thru his cross.

Rise to greet the sun

27

Tzu-ch`en, Chao, 1931
English trans., Mildred A. Wiant,
Bliss Wiant, 1936

trad. Chinese melody
arr., Bliss Wiant, 1936

1. Rise to greet the sun, red - dening in the sky,
2. Fa - ther, I im - plore, safe - ly keep this child;
3. May this day be blest; trust - ing Je - sus' love,

war - rior - like and strong, come - ly as a groom;
make my con - duct good, ac - tions calm and mild:
my heart's freed from ill; fair blue sky's a - bove.

birds pass high in flight, fra - grant flowers now bloom;
ven - er - at - ing age, hum - bly teach - ing youth,
Glad for cot - ton coat, plain food sat - is - fies;

with the gra - cious light I my toil re - sume.
al - ways serv - ing thee, shar - ing thy rich truth.
all my count - less needs thy kind hand sup - plies.

28 It may not be on the mountain
I'll go where you want me to go

Mary Brown, 1892

Carrie E. Rounsefell, 1894

1. It may not be on the moun - tain height, or
2. Per - haps to - day there are lov - ing words which
3. There's sure - ly some - where a low - ly place in

o - ver the storm - y sea, it may not be at the
Je - sus would have me speak; there may be now in the
earth's har - vest fields so wide, where I may la - bor thro'

bat - tle's front my Lord will have need of me; but
paths of sin some wan - d'rer whom I should seek: O
life's short day for Je - sus, the Cru - ci - fied; so

if, by a still, small voice he calls to
Sav - ior, if thou wilt be my guide, tho'
trust - ing my all to thy ten - der care, and

paths that I do not know, I'll an-swer, dear Lord, with my
dark and rug-ged the way, my voice shall ech-o the
know-ing thou lov - est me, I'll do thy will with a

hand in thine, I'll go where you want me to go.
mes - sage sweet, I'll say what you want me to say.
heart sin - cere, I'll be what you want me to be.

Refrain

I'll go where you want me to go, dear Lord, o - ver

moun-tain, or plain, or sea; I'll say what you want me to

say, dear Lord. I'll be what you want me to be.

29

Momento novo
In this new moment

words and music, Ernesto Barros, Darlene Schützer,
Paulo R. Selles, Tércio Junker,
Dea C. Affini, Eder Soares

harm., Daniel Charles Damon

Marcha Rancho

Portuguese:
1. Deus cha - ma a gen - te pra'um mo - men - to
2. Não é pos - sí - vel crer que tu - do é
3. A for - ça que ho - je faz bro - tar a

no - vo de ca - mi - nhar jun - to com seu
fá - cil, há mui - ta for - ça que pro - duz a
vi - da, a - tu - a em nós pe - la su - a

no - vo É ho - ra de trans - for - mar o
mor - te. Ge - ran - do dor, tris - te - za e
gra - ça, é Deus quem nos con - vi - da

que não dá mais; so - zi - nho, i - so - la - do, nin -
de - so - la - ção; é ne - ces - sá - rio u -
pra tra - ba - lhar, o a - mor re - par - tir e as

guém é ca - paz!
nir o cor - dão! Por is - so, vem,
for - ças jun - tar.

Coro

en - tra na ro - da co'a gen - te! Tam -

bém vo - cê é mui - to im - por -

1. tan - te. Por is - so, 2. tan - te. Vem!

30

In this new moment
Momento novo

words and music, Ernesto Barros, Darlene
Schützer, Paulo R. Selles, Tércio Junker,
Dea C. Affini, Eder Soares
English trans., Daniel Charles Damon

harm., Daniel Charles Damon

Marcha Rancho

1. In this new mo - ment we can hear God
2. Do not as - sume that life is e - ver
3. There is a lov - ing force that now e -

call - ing; in this new time, all shall walk to -
ea - sy, for in this world there are dead - ly
mer - ges; a gift of grace, bind - ing us to -

geth - er. In this new mo - ment we learn to
for - ces, and in this life there is pain, des -
geth - er; for it is God who in - vites each

change what is wrong, though no one is a - ble to
truc - tion, and fear. Let this be the mo - ment to
one to the work, to share what we have in the

31

Sois la semilla
You are the seed

Cesáreo Gabaraín, 1979
trans., Raquel Gutiérrez-Achón
and Skinner Chávez-Melo

Cesáreo Gabaraín, 1979
harm., Skinner Chávez-Melo, 1987

1. Sois la se - mi - lla que ha de cre - cer, sois es-
Sois la ma - ña - na que vuel - ve a na - cer, sois es-

1. You are the seed that will grow a new sprout; you're a
You are the dawn that will bring a new day; you're the

tre - lla que ha de bri - llar.
pi - ga que em-pie - za a gra - nar.

star that will shine in the night;
wheat that will bear gold-en grain;

Sois le - va - du - ra, sois
Sois a - gui - jón y ca-

you are the yeast and a
you are a sting and a

gra - no de sal, an - tor - cha que de - be a lum - brar.
ri - cia a la vez, tes - ti - gos que voy a en - viar.

small grain of salt, a bea-con to glow in the dark.
soft, gen-tle touch, my wit-ness - es wher-e'er you go.

2.
Sois una llama que ha de encender
resplandores de fe y caridad.
Sois los pastores que han de llevar
al mundo por sendas de paz.
Sois los amigos que quise escoger,
sois palabra que intento esparcir.
Sois reino nuevo que empieza a engendrar
justicia, amor y verdad.
Estribillo

3.
Sois fuego y savia que vine a traer,
sois la ola que agita la mar.
La levadura pequeña de ayer
fermenta la masa del pan.
Una ciudad no se puede esconder,
ni los montes se han de ocultar,
en vuestras obras que buscan el bien
el mundo al Padre verá.
Estribillo

2.
You are the flame that will lighten the dark,
sending sparkles of hope, faith, and love;
you are the shepherds to lead the whole world
through valleys and pastures of peace.
You are the friends that I chose for myself,
the word that I want to proclaim.
You are the new kingdom built on a rock
where justice and truth always reign.
Refrain

3.
You are the life that will nurture the plant;
you're the waves in a turbulent sea;
yesterday's yeast is beginning to rise,
a new loaf of bread it will yield.
There is no place for a city to hide,
nor a mountain can cover its might;
may your good deeds show a world in despair
a path that will lead all to God.
Refrain

32 Te ofrecemos padre nuestro
Let us offer to the Father

De la Misa Popular Nicaragüense
trans., Alice Parker, 1994

De la Misa Popular Nicaragüense
arr., Raquel Mora Martínez, 1994

Estribillo/Refrain

Te o-fre - ce - mos, Pa - dre nues - tro, con el
Let us of - fer to the Fa - ther with the

vi - no y con el pan nues-tras pe - nas y a - le -
bread and with the wine all our joys and all our

Fine

grí - as,___ el tra - ba - jo y nues - tro a fán.
sor - rows:___ all our cares, Lord, all are thine.

1. Co - mo el tri - go de los cam - pos en un
2. A los po - bres de la tie - rra, a los
1. As the grow - ing wheat will ri - pen let us
2. Let the poor and hea - vy la - den gath - er

pan	se	con -	vir - tió		a -	sí	haz	de nues -	tras
que	su -	frien -	do es - tán,		cam -	bia	su	do - lor	en
show	to	all	the world		we	can	grow	and ri -	pen
at	the	Sa -	vior's sign		where	their	grief	will turn	to

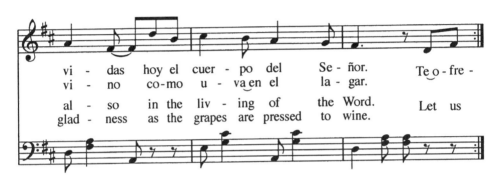

vi -	das	hoy el	cuer - po	del	Se -	ñor.	Te o - fre -
vi -	no	co-mo	u - va en	el	la -	gar.	
al -	so	in the	liv - ing	of	the	Word.	Let us
glad -	ness	as the	grapes are	pressed	to	wine.	

3. Estos dones son el signo
   del esfuerzo de unidad
   que la humanidad realiza
   en el campo y la ciudad.

4. Es tu pueblo quien te ofrece
   con los dones del altar
   la naturaleza entera
   anhelando libertad.

5. Gloria sea dada al Padre
   y a su Hijo Redentor,
   y al Espíritu Divino
   que nos llena de su amor.

3. From the country, from the city,
   from the riches of the land,
   we bring back to our Creator
   many gifts of heart and hand.

4. All your people here together
   bring you offerings of love,
   joining with your whole creation
   seeking liberty and peace.

5. Glory be to God, the Father
   and to Christ, the living Son,
   who together with the Spirit
   make the Holy Three in One.

33 Canção da caminhada
If walking is our vocation

words and music, Simei Monteiro
English trans., Jaci Maraschin, alt.

Portuguese:
1. Se ca - mi - nhar é pre - ci - so,
e nos - sos pés, nos - sos bra - ços,
2. Se ca - mi - nhar é pre - ci - so,
e nos - sa fé se - rá tan - ta

English:
1. If walk - ing is our vo - ca - tion,
and on this jour - ney our foot - steps
2. If walk - ing is our vo - ca - tion,
Our faith will be great and glor - ious

1. ca - mi - nha - re - mos u - ni - dos
sus - ten - ta - rão nos - sos pas - sos.
2. ca - mi - nha - re - mos u - ni - dos
que trans - po - rá as mon - ta - nhas.

1. sure - ly we'll walk with each oth - er
will be sus - tained by our bod - ies.
2. sure - ly we'll walk with each oth - er.
and it will move e - ven moun - tains.

1. Não mais se - re - mos a mas - sa sem vez, sem
2. Va - mos a - brin - do fron - tei - ras on - de só ha-

1. We'll be no long - er like noth - ing with - out a
2. We'll o - pen fron - tiers of chal - lenge re - mov - ing

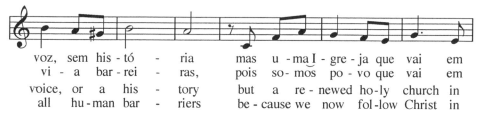

voz, sem his - tó - ria mas u - ma I - gre - ja que vai em
vi - a bar - rei - ras, pois so - mos po - vo que vai em

voice, or a his - tory but a re - newed ho - ly church in
all hu - man bar - riers be - cause we now fol - low Christ in

es - pe - ran-ça   so - li - dá -   ria.
es - pe - ran-ça   so - li - dá -   ria.

hope and joy-ful   sol - i - dar - i - ty.
hope and joy-ful   sol - i - dar - i - ty.

3. Se caminhar é preciso, caminharemos unidos,
   e o Reino de Deus teremos como horizonte de vida.
   Compartiremos as dores, os sofrimentos e as penas
   levando a força do amor em esperança solidária.

4. Se caminhar é preciso, caminharemos unidos
   e nossa voz no deserto fará brotar novas fontes.
   E a nova vida na terra será antevista nas festas.
   É Deus que está entre nós em esperança solidária.

3. If walking is our vocation, surely we'll walk with each other.
   Of all our visions God's Kingdom will be our only horizon.
   We will be sharing our sorrows, our vile oppression and sufferings,
   bearing together our love in hope and joyful solidarity.

4. If walking is our vocation, surely we'll walk with each other.
   Alone our voice in the desert in awe will bring forth new fountains,
   and the new life in this planet a feast is anticipating.
   God is alive in our midst in hope and joyful solidarity.

34 Here I am, Lord

words and music, Dan Schutte, 1981   arr., Carlton R. Young, 1988

35 Eternal God, whose power upholds

Henry H. Tweedy, 1929

Rhys Thomas, 1929

1. E - ter - nal God, whose power up - holds, both
2. O God of love, whose Spir - it wakes in
3. O God of truth, whom sci - ence seeks and
4. O God of beau - ty, oft re - vealed in
5. O God of right - eous - ness and grace, seen

flower and flam - ing star, to whom there is no
ev - 'ry hu - man breast, whom love, and love a -
rev - 'rent souls a - dore, who light - est ev - 'ry
dreams of hu - man art, in speech that flows to
in the Christ, thy Son, whose life and death re -

here nor there, no time, no near nor far, no
lone can know, in whom all hearts find rest, help
earn - est mind of ev - 'ry clime and shore, dis -
mel - o - dy, in ho - li - ness of heart, teach
veal thy face, by whom thy will was done, in -

a - lien race, no for - eign shore, no child un -
us to spread thy gra - cious reign till greed and
pel the gloom of er - ror's night, of ig - no -
spire thy her - alds of good news to live thy

sought, un - known, Oh! send us forth, thy
hate shall cease, and kind - ness dwell in
rance and fear, un - til true wis - dom
life di - vine, till Christ is formed in

proph - ets true, to make all lands thine own!
hu - man hearts, and all the earth find peace!
from a - bove shall make life's path - way clear!
love - li - ness of lives made fair and free.
hu - man - kind and ev - 'ry land is thine!

36 Your Spirit, God, moves us to pray

Mary Nelson Keithahn, 1996

John Horman, 1996

1. Your Spir - it, God, moves us to pray for chil - dren in the world to - day whose on - ly home may be the street, who nev - er have e - nough to eat,
2. Your Spir - it, God, moves us to pray for chil - dren in the world to - day whose tongues must learn new ways to talk, who can - not see or hear or walk,
3. Kind, gen - tle God, this is our prayer: that we might learn to love and share the bless - ings that you show - er down, a lov - ing home, a friend - ly town,

37

Oré poriajú verekó
O Lord, have mercy

Guaraní Kyrie, Paraguay
harm., Carlton R. Young
obbligato, Pablo Sosa

trad. Guaraní liturgical text

obbligato for soprano or instrument

Oo

Guaraní: O - ré po-ria-jú ve-re-kó, Ñan-de
Greek: Ky-ri - e e-le-i-son, ky-ri - e e-le-i-
Chri - ste e-le-i-son, Chri - ste e-le-i-

English: O Lord, have mer - cy, O Lord, have
O Christ, have mer - cy, O Christ, have

ya - ra; O - ré po-ria - jú ve-re-
son, ky-ri - e e-le-i-son, ky-ri-
son, Chri - ste e-le-i-son, Chri -

mer - cy, O Lord, have mer - cy, have
mer - cy, O Christ have mer - cy, have

kó, Ñan - de - ya - - ra.
e   e - le - i - son.
ste   e - le - i - son.
mer - cy on us.
mer - cy on us.

Gospodi pomilui 38
Lord, have mercy
Kyrie eleison

Russian Orthodox chant

Russian translit.: Gos - po - di po - mi - lui, Gos - po - di po - mi - lui.
English: Lord, have mer - cy on us. Lord, have mer - cy on us.
Greek: Ky - ri - e e - lei - son, ky - ri - e e - lei - son.

Kyrie 39
Lord, have mercy

liturgical text

Dinah Reindorf

Greek: Ky - ri - e e - le - i - son. Ky - ri - e e - le - i - son.
English: Lord, have mer - cy on us. Lord, have mer - cy on us.

Ky - ri - e e - le - i - son. Ky - ri - e e - le - i - son.
Lord, have mer - cy on us. Lord, have mer - cy on us.

40

Du är helig
You are holy

words and music, Per Harling, 1990

Part 1 (may be sung as a canon)

Swedish: Du är he - lig, Du är hel,
English: You are ho - ly, you are whole,

Du är all - tid myck - et mer, än vi
you are al - ways ev - er more than we

nån - sin kan för - stå. Du är nä - ra än - då.
ev - er un - der - stand, you are al - ways at hand.

Väl - sig - nad va - re Du, Som
Bless - ed are you com - ing near, bless - ed

The church of Christ, in every age **41**

Fred Pratt Green, 1969

Lee Hastings Bristol, Jr., 1962

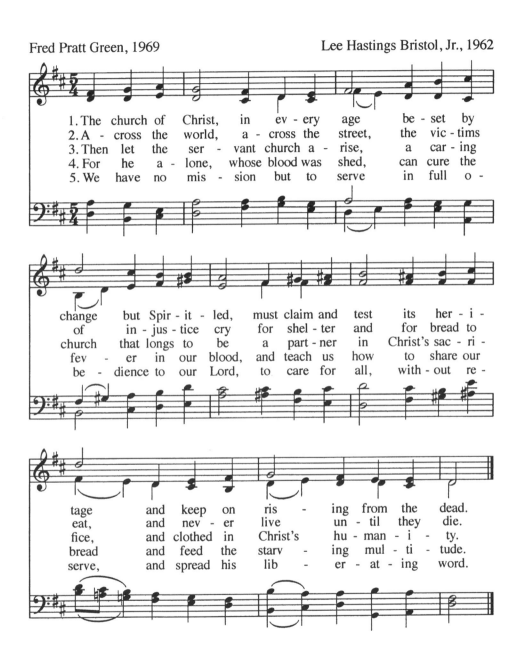

1. The church of Christ, in ev - ery age be - set by
2. A - cross the world, a - cross the street, the vic - tims
3. Then let the ser - vant church a - rise, a car - ing
4. For he a - lone, whose blood was shed, can cure the
5. We have no mis - sion but to serve in full o -

change but Spir - it - led, must claim and test its her - i -
of in - jus - tice cry for shel - ter and for bread to
church that longs to be a part - ner in Christ's sac - ri -
fev - er in our blood, and teach us how to share our
be - dience to our Lord, to care for all, with - out re -

tage and keep on ris - ing from the dead.
eat, and nev - er live un - til they die.
fice, and clothed in Christ's hu - man - i - ty.
bread and feed the starv - ing mul - ti - tude.
serve, and spread his lib - er - at - ing word.

42 Here am I

words and music, Nolan Williams, Jr., b. 1968

1. God has no hands but those that strive to mend the bro-ken hearts of wound-ed kin, God has no feet but those that stride to
2. God has no eyes but those a-lert to see some-one dis-tressed, some soul in need, God has no voice un-less we yield to
3. God's call is now for us to build and keep the liv-ing Church, Christ's Bride to be, so we must work the work and sow the

There's a Spirit in the air 43

Medieval French melody
harm., Richard Redhead, 1853

Brian Wren, 1969/1989

1. There's a Spir - it in the air, tell - ing
2. Lose your shy - ness, find your tongue; tell the
3. When be - liev - ers break the bread, when a
4. Still the Spir - it gives us light, see - ing
5. When a stran - ger's not a - lone, where the
6. May the Spir - it fill our praise, guide our
7. There's a Spir - it in the air, call - ing

Chris - tians ev - ery - where: "Praise the love that
world what God has done: God in Christ has
hun - gry child is fed, praise the love that
wrong and set - ting right: God in Christ has
home - less find a home, praise the love that
thoughts and change our ways. God in Christ has
peo - ple ev - ery - where: Praise the love that

Christ re - vealed, liv - ing, work - ing, in our world."
come to stay. Live to - mor - row's life to - day!
Christ re - vealed, liv - ing, work - ing, in our world.
come to stay. Live to - mor - row's life to - day!
Christ re - vealed, liv - ing, work - ing, in our world.
come to stay. Live to - mor - row's life to - day!
Christ re - vealed, liv - ing, work - ing, in our world.

44 Whose child is this?

S T Kimbrough, Jr., 1997   S T Kimbrough, Jr., Timothy Kimbrough, 1997

Verse text (under music):

1. Whose child is this? I ask, a child you've
   Whose child is this? I see a child you've
2. Whose child is this, who cries and stum - bles
   "Whose child," I ask, "is this, who lives in
3. Whose child is this?— black, red, white, yel - low,
   Once Je - sus said, "Let all the chil - dren

nev - er known? Is it too great a
al - ways known. How strange it is to
in the street, who trem - bles as he
wealth and ease, who nev - er feels a
bronze, or brown, born with - out rac - ists'
come to me." If you would heed this

Advent/Christmas:

4. "Whose child is this," I ask
   "who comes at Christmas time,
   bringing a love to earth
   that makes all life sublime?"
A child in whom all children see
the kind of love that makes them free
to be what they are meant to be.

Refrain:
Each child is God's child, yours, and mine.
Christ is a gift of love divine.

rit.

out - stretched arms, will you be there?
make her lone - ly spir - it sing?
bathe your feet, the pain al - lay."
she be forced such love to earn?
love, God's love, the world is freed!
Sav - ior bids you love them too.

Refrain *a tempo*

Each child is God's child, yours, and mine.
*(This)

You are a gift of love di - vine.
*(Christ is)

*Words in parenthesis are for Advent/Christmas stanza.

This is the day

45

words and music T. Janet Surdam, 1953

arr., Esther B. Stockwell

This is the day, this is the day. This is the day that the
Lord hath made. Let us re-joice in it. Let us re-
joice in it. Let us re-joice in it and be glad. This is the
day, this is the day. This is the day that the
Lord hath made. Let us re-joice in it and be glad.

46 Ye servants of God

Charles Wesley, 1744

Lim Swee Hong, 1999

Jubilant

1. Ye ser - vants of God, your Mas - ter pro-
2. God rul - eth on high, al - might - y to
3. "Sal - va - tion to God, who sits on the
4. Then let us a - dore and give him his

claim, and pub - lish a - broad his won - der - ful
save, and still he is nigh, his pre - sence we
throne!" Let all cry a - loud and hon - or the
right, all glo - ry and power, all wis - dom and

Performance Note: Use the keyboard accompaniment as a basis of your improvisation. Sense the energy of the music rather than the precise count of the note values.

name; the name all vic - to - rious of
have; the great con - gre - ga - tion his
Son; the prais - es of Je - sus the
might; all hon - or and bless - ing with

Je - sus ex - tol, his king - dom is
tri - umph shall sing, as - crib - ing sal -
an - gels pro - claim, fall down on their
an - gels a - bove, and thanks nev - er

glo - rious and rules o - ver all.
va - tion to Je - sus, our King.
fac - es and wor - ship the Lamb.
ceas - ing and in - fi - nite love.

Refrain

Hal - le! Hal - le - lu - jah! Hal - le!

1. Hal - le! Hal - le - lu - jah!

2. Hal - le! Hal - le - lu - jah!

What does the Lord require 47

Albert F. Bayly, 1949

Erik Routley, 1968

1. What does the Lord re - quire for praise and
2. Rul - ers of earth, give ear! Should you not
3. All who gain wealth by trade, for whom the
4. How shall our life ful - fill God's law so

of - fer - ing? What sac - ri - fice, de - sire, or trib - ute
jus - tice know? Will God your plead - ing hear, while crime and
work - er toils, think not to win God's aid, if greed your
hard and high? Let Christ en - due our will with grace to

bid you bring? Do just - ly; love mer - cy; walk
cruel - ty grow? Do just - ly; love mer - cy; walk
com - merce soils. Do just - ly; love mer - cy; walk
for - ti - fy. Then just - ly, in mer - cy, we'll

1. 2. 3.

hum - bly with your God.
hum - bly with your God.
hum - bly with your God.

4.

hum - bly walk with God.

48 Tenemos esperanza
We have hope

Federico J. Pagura
trans., George Lockwood

Homero R. Perera

on 3rd stanza go to CODA

1. Por - que Él en -
1. Be - cause Christ

tró en el mun-do y en la his - to - ria; por-que Él que-
came to en - ter in our jour-ney, be -cause he

bró el si - len-cio y la a - go - ní - a; por-que lle-
broke the si - lence of our sor - row, be - cause he

nó la tie - rra de su glo - ria; por - que fue
filled the whole world with his glo - ry, and came to

luz en nues-tra no-che frí - a; por-que Él na-
light the dark-ness of our mor - row. Be - cause he

cíó en un pe - se - bre os-cu - ro; por-que Él vi-
came a stran-ger poor and low - ly, be - cause he

vió sem-bran-do a - mor y vi - da; por - que par-
lived, pro-claim-ing love and heal - ing, be - cause he

tió los co - ra - zo - nes du - ros y le - van-
o - pened hearts of hun-gry peo - ple, and brought new

CODA   Estribillo/Refrain

tó las al - mas a - ba - ti - das. Por
life to all who would re - ceive it. In

2. Porque atacó a ambiciosos mercaderes
   y denunció maldad e hipocresía;
   porque exaltó a los niños, las mujeres,
   y rechazó a los que de orgullo ardían.
   Porque Él cargó la cruz de nuestras penas
   y saboreó la hiel de nuestros males;
   porque aceptó sufrir nuestra condena
   y así morir por todos los mortales.

3. Porque una aurora vió su gran victoria
   sobre la muerte, el miedo, las mentiras,
   ya nada puede detener su historia,
   ni de su Reino eterno la venida.
   to CODA

2. Because he dealt with all the angry merchants
   and he declared the evil of their doings,
   because he lifted every child and woman
   and put aside the proud and hateful people,
   because he bore a cross for all our sorrow
   and knew our every weakness and temptation,
   because he took the pain of condemnation
   and then he died for every kind of person.

3. Because his triumph came one early morning
   and he defeated death and fear and sorrow,
   because he moved triumphant to the future
   to bring a Kingdom saving all tomorrow.
   to CODA

This land of beauty

49

words and music, Elena G. Maquiso

1. This land of beauty has been given by
2. The self-ish peo-ple and not mind-ful, the
3. The far-mer longs for whole-some liv-ing with
4. Poor farm-ers have a right to this land. Pos-

God our Fa-ther, full of mer-cy. Its
few, will claim the land to own. De-
food to eat and e-nough cloth-ing, a
ses-sion ac-cents their well-be-ing. For

love-li-ness has been in-tend-ed for
prive the man-y poor and need-y who
bet-ter house, to live in com-fort with
here are hopes for bright-er fu-tures, a

ev-ery one and all the peo-ple, and
live in want and al-ways suf-fer. And
things to use in-side the dwel-ling, his
bet-ter life, re-ward for striv-ing. And

each one claims the right-ful por-tion, a
when this hap-pens there is con-flict, for
child to have a bright to-mor-row, when
to the wealth-y, we im-plore you vast

piece of land one proud-ly owns. This her-i-tage so full of
hate and bit-ter-ness pre-vail. Re-la-tion-ships will be found
he can pro-vide ed-u-ca-tion. Pa-ren-tal hap-pi-ness his
por-tions of your land to share. The poor have more need for it,

prom-ise, this land was pur-posed for us all.
want-ing and hap-pi-ness will pass them by.
feel-ing and kind-ly neigh-bor's love a-round.
tru-ly; the right to land is for us all.

50 God of our foremothers
Make plain the vision

Shirley Erena Murray, 1998

Carlton R. Young, 1998

Gentle waltz

1. God of our fore-moth-ers, God of our day, fir - ing, in-spir-ing our song.
2. Spir - it who chal -leng- es all that we see, widen-ing our screen to your scope—
3. Ours is the role and the work of the soul, each in our ev-ery-day place

wo - man's own voice call - ing for free - dom from wrong:
tug - ging our hand, need - ing di - rec - tion and hope.
vi - si - ble sign, in - ward and spir - it - ual grace.

God who is wis - dom, in
new gen-er - a - tions are
prov - ing by out - ward and

51 Do not wait until some deed

Brighten the corner where you are

Ina D. Ogdon, 1913

Charles H. Gabriel, 1921

1. Do not wait un - til some deed of great - ness
2. Just a - bove are cloud - ed skies that you may
3. Here for all your ta - lent you may sure - ly

you may do, do not wait to shed your light a - far, to the
help to clear, let not nar - row self your way de - bar, though in -
find a need, here re - flect the bright and morn - ing star; e - ven

man - y du - ties ev - er near you now be true,
to one heart a - lone may fall your song of cheer,
from your hum - ble hand the bread of life may feed,

bright - en the cor - ner where you are.
bright - en the cor - ner where you are.
bright - en the cor - ner where you are.

Refrain

Bright-en the cor-ner where you are!

Shine for Je - sus where you are!

Bright - en the cor - ner where you are!

Some-one far from har - bor you may guide a - cross the bar.

Bright - en the cor - ner where you are!

52 Hallelu, Christ is risen

Charles Wesley
refrain, S T Kimbough, Jr.

S T Kimbrough, Jr. 2001
arr., Mary K. Jackson

Refrain

Hal - le-lu, Christ is ris - en! Now the stone's rolled a - way.

Fine

Hal - le-lu, Christ is ris - en! Pro-claim the news to-day!

1. More cou - ra - geous than the men, when
2. Wo - men first the news pro - claim, know
3. Joy - ful tid - ings of their Lord these
4. O might I like them now hear, these

53   Every day

Shirley Erena Murray, 1992   Colin Gibson, 1993

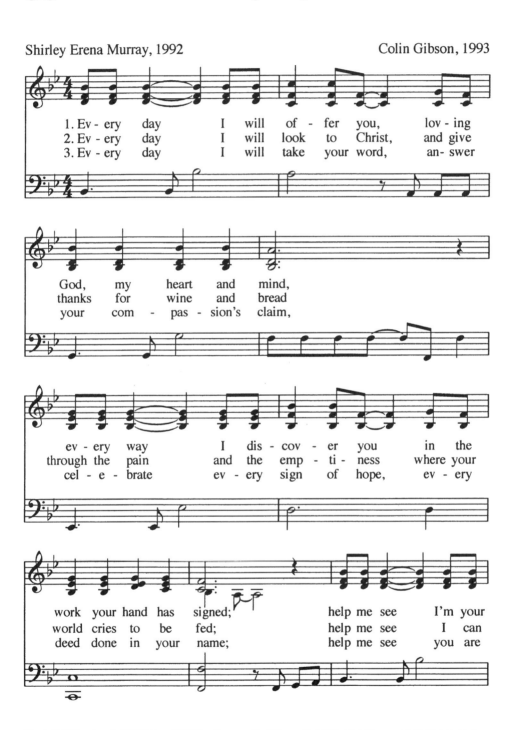

1. Ev - ery day   I will of - fer you,   lov - ing
2. Ev - ery day   I will look to Christ,   and give
3. Ev - ery day   I will take your word,   an- swer

God, my heart and mind,
thanks for wine and bread
your com - pas - sion's claim,

ev - ery way   I dis - cov - er you   in the
through the pain   and the emp - ti - ness   where your
cel - e - brate   ev - ery sign of hope,   ev - ery

work your hand has signed;   help me see   I'm your
world cries to be fed;   help me see   I can
deed done in your name;   help me see   you are

im - age, and you have dreamed what I might be,
work for change, and wher - ev - er I might be,
al - ways there, and your light can shine through me,

ev - ery day in your Spir - it I'll find the love and
ev - ery day in your Spir - it I'll find the love and
ev - ery day in your Spir - it I'll find the love and

1.2.
en – er – gy
en – er – gy!
en – er –

3.
gy!

54 Tú has venido a la orilla
Lord, when you came to the seashore

words and music, Cesáreo Gabaraín, 1979   arr., Skinner Chávez-Melo, 1987

1. Tú has ve-ni-do a la o-ri - lla, no has bus-ca - do ni a sa-bios ni a ri - cos tan só - lo quie - res que yo te si - ga y mi tra-ba - jo. Se - ñor,

2. Tú sa-bes bien lo que ten - go: en mi bar - ca no hay o - ro ni es-pa - das, tan só - lo re - des y mi tra-ba - jo. Se - ñor,

3. Tú ne-ce-si-tas mis ma - nos, mi can-san - cio que a o - tros des-can - se, a - mor que quie - ra se-guir a-man - do.

4. Tú pes-ca-dor de o-tros ma - res, an - sia e-ter - na de al-mas que es-pe - ran, a - mi-go bue - no, que a - sí me lla - mas.

Estribillo

55 Lord, when you came to the seashore
Tú has venido a la orilla

words and music, Cesáreo Gabaraín, 1979
English text, Willard F. Jabusch

arr., Skinner Chávez-Melo, 1987

1. Lord, when you came to the sea - shore
2. Lord, you knew what my boat car - ried;
3. Lord, have you need of my la - bor,
4. Lord, send me where you would have me,

you weren't seek - ing the wise or the
nei - ther mon - ey nor weap - ons for
hands for ser - vice, a heart made for
to a vill - age, or heart of the

wealth - y, but on - ly ask - ing
fight - ing, but nets for fish - ing
lov - ing, my arms for lift - ing
ci - ty; I will re - mem - ber

Refrain

__ that I might fol - low.
__ my dai - ly la - bor.
__ the poor and bro - ken?
__ that you are with me.

O Lord,

56

El cielo canta alegría
Heaven is singing for joy

words and music, Pablo Sosa, 1991

Spanish: El cie-lo can-ta a-le-grí-a, ¡A-le-lu - ya!
English: Heav-en is sing-ing for joy, al-le-lu - ia!

1. Por - que en tu vi - da y la mí - a bri - lla la
2. Por - que a tu vi - da y la mí - a las u - ne el
3. Por - que tu vi - da y la mí - a pro - cla - ma-

1. For in your life and in mine is shin - ing the
2. For your life and mine u - nite in the
3. For your life and mine will al - ways bear

glo - ria de Dios.
a - mor de Dios.
rán al Se - ñor.

glo - ry of God.
love of the Lord.
wit - ness to God.

Estribillo/Refrain

¡A - le - lu - ya!
Al - le - lu - ia!

¡A - le - lu - ya!
Al - le - lu - ia!

¡A - le -
Al - le -

lu - ya!   ¡A - le - lu - ya!
lu - ia!   Al - le - lu - ia!

My country 'tis for thee   57

words, anon.

Thesaurus Musicus, 1744

1. My coun - try 'tis for thee, dark land of
2. From ev - ery moun - tain side, up - on the
3. Our fa - thers' God, to thee, au - thor of

slav - er - y, for thee I weep; land where the
o - cean's tide, they call on thee; a - mid thy
li - ber - ty, to thee we pray; soon may our

slave has sighed, and where he toiled and died,
rocks and rills, thy woods and tem - pled hills,
land be pure, let free - dom's light en - dure,

to serve a ty - rant's pride, for thee I weep.
I hear a voice which trills— let all go free.
and lib - er - ty se - cure, be - neath thy sway.

58 As a fire is meant for burning

The Sacred Harp, 1844
arr., Ronald A. Nelson, 1978

Ruth Duck, 1992

1. As a fire is meant for burn-ing with a bright and warm-ing
2. We are learn-ers; we are teach-ers; we are pil-grims on the
3. As a green bud in the spring-time is a sign of life re-

flame, so the church is meant for mis-sion, giv-ing
way. We are seek-ers; we are giv-ers; we are
newed, so may we be signs of one-ness 'mid earth's

glo-ry to God's name. Not to preach our creeds or
ves-sels made of clay. By our gen-tle, lov-ing
peo-ples, man-y hued. As a rain-bow lights the

cus-toms, but to build a bridge of care, we join
ac-tions we would show that Christ is light. In a
heav-ens when a storm is past and gone, may our

hands a-cross the na - tions, find-ing neigh-bors ev - ery-where.
hum - ble, lis- tening Spir - it we would live to God's de - light.
lives re - flect the ra - diance of God's new and glo - rious dawn.

Nurtured by the Spirit* 59

words and music, Per Harling, 2000

Nur-tured by the Spir - it, walk-ing in God's light we are
o-pen to the vi-sion from a - bove. Shar - ing fruits of heav - en,
car - ing for the right we will walk with the mis - sion of
love. We are the seeds, sown in weak-ness, raised in
power, God, make us sprout. We are in need of your
Spir - it, now's the hour: God, send us out!

* May be sung as a canon.

60 Brich mit den Hungrigen dein Brot
Break with the hungry your own bread

Friedrich Karl Barth
English trans., S T Kimbrough, Jr.

Peter Janssens, 1977

German: 1. Brich mit den Hun-gri-gen dein Brot, sprich mit den
2. Such mit den Fer-ti-gen ein Ziel, brich mit den
3. Teil mit den Ein-sa-men dein Haus, such mit den

English: 1. Break with the hun-gry your own bread. Speak with the
2. Seek with the hope-less a new goal. Break with the
3. Share with the lone-ly your own house. Seek with the

Sprach-lo-sen ein Wort, sing mit den Trau-ri-gen ein
Hun-gri-gen dein Brot, sprich mit den Sprach-los-en ein
Fer-ti-gen ein Ziel brich mit den Hun-gri-gen dein

speech-less a kind word. Sing with the sor-row-ful a
hun-gry your own bread. Speak with the speech-less a kind
hope-less a new goal. Break with the hun-gry your own

Lied, teil mit den Ein-sam-en dein Haus.
Wort, sing mit den Trau-ri-gen ein Lied.
Brot, sprich mit den Sprach-lo-sen ein Wort.

song. Share with the lone-ly your own house.
word. Sing with the sor-row-ful a song.
bread. Speak with the speech-less a kind word.

4. Sing mit den Traurigen ein Lied,
   teil mit den Einsamen dein Haus,
   such mit den Fertigen ein Ziel,
   brich mit den Hungrigen dein Brot.

5. Sprich mit den Sprachlosen ein Wort,
   sing mit den Traurigen ein Lied,
   teil mit den Einsamen dein Haus,
   such mit den Fertigen ein Ziel.

4. Sing with the sorrowful a song.
   Share with the lonely your own house.
   Seek with the hopeless a new goal.
   Break with the hungry your own bread.

5. Speak with the speechless a kind word.
   Sing with the sorrowful a song.
   Share with the lonely your own house.
   Seek with the hopeless a new goal.

Yarabba ssalami
O, God of peace

61

author unknown

trad. Palestinian melody
arr. Arne Lundmark, 2004

Arabic: Ya - ra - bba ssa - la - mi am - ter a-lay - na sa-lam, ya - ra - bba ssa la - mi im la qu - lu - ba - na sa-lam.

English: O, God of peace, send down your peace on our world. O God of peace, fill our hearts with your peace.

62 Children from your vast creation

David A. Robb, 1996

The Sacred Harp, 1844
harm., Alfred V. Fedak, 1994

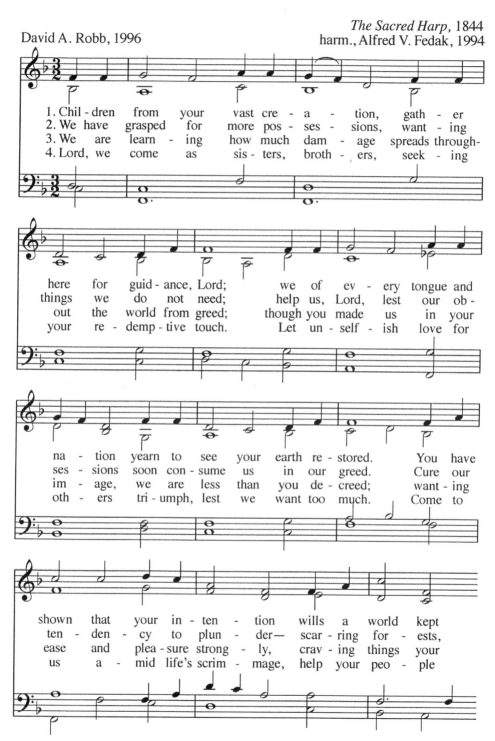

1. Chil - dren from your vast cre - a - tion, gath - er
2. We have grasped for more pos - ses - sions, want - ing
3. We are learn - ing how much dam - age spreads through-
4. Lord, we come as sis - ters, broth - ers, seek - ing

here for guid - ance, Lord; we of ev - ery tongue and
things we do not need; help us, Lord, lest our ob -
out the world from greed; though you made us in your
your re - demp - tive touch. Let un - self - ish love for

na - tion yearn to see your earth re - stored. You have
ses - sions soon con - sume us in our greed. Cure our
im - age, we are less than you de - creed; want - ing
oth - ers tri - umph, lest we want too much. Come to

shown that your in - ten - tion wills a world kept
ten - den - cy to plun - der— scar - ring for - ests,
ease and plea - sure strong - ly, crav - ing things your
us a - mid life's scrim - mage, help your peo - ple

free from strife; o - pen us to love's di -
wast - ing ore; come, and turn our schemes a -
love de - plores, ask - ing not, or ask - ing
live as one: re - cre - ate us in your

men - sion filled with true a - bun - dant life.
sun - der; take a - way our lust for more.
wrong - ly, we re - sort to wag - ing wars.
im - age; speed the day your will is done!

Come, let us seek our God's protection 63

Tom Colvin, 1997   Malawian folk song, adapt., Tom Colvin, 1997

Leader*

1. Come, let us seek our God's pro - tect - tion,
2. Our foes are gath - ered all a - round us,
3. See fear, des - pair and guilt en - slave us,
4. Our eyes are tired from too much weep - ing,
5. God knows our suf - fering, sees our trou - ble,
6. God is our ref - uge and de - fend - er,
7. How won - der - ful God's con - stant love is,
8. Our God u - nites us as one peo - ple,
9. Let's dance and sing to God our Sav - ior,
10. And shout for joy with all God's chil - dren,
11. Ha - le - lu - ya, yes, ha - le - lu - ya,

All

Ye-su sets us free to love and serve, Ye-su sets us free.

*All hum during the stanzas which are sung by a leader, or two people singing alternately.

64 Heralds of Christ

Laura S. Copenhaver, 1915

George W. Warren, 1894

Trumpets, before each stanza

1. Her - alds of Christ, who
2. Through des - ert ways, dark
3. Lord, give us faith and

bear the King's com - mands,
fen, and deep mo - rass,
strength the road to build,

im - mor - tal tid - ings
through jun - gles, slug - gish
to see the prom - ise

in your mor - tal hands,
seas, and moun-tain pass,
of the day ful - filled,

pass on and car - ry
build now the road, and
when war shall be no

swift the news you bring;
fal - ter not, nor stay;
more, and strife shall cease

make straight, make
pre - pare a -
up - on the

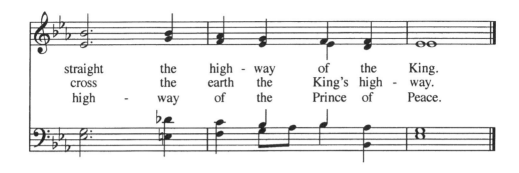

straight   the   high - way   of   the   King.
cross   the   earth   the   King's high - way.
high - way   of   the   Prince   of   Peace.

Jesus still lives

65

words and music, Suzanne Toolan, SM, 1985

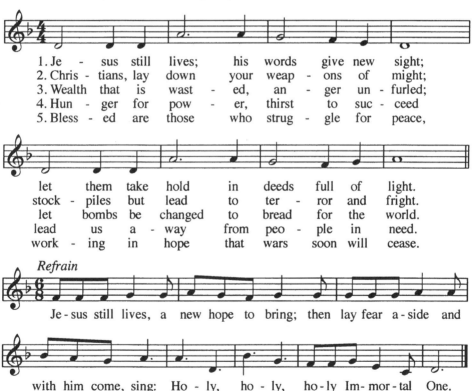

1. Je - sus still lives; his words give new sight;
2. Chris - tians, lay down your weap - ons of might;
3. Wealth that is wast - ed, an - ger un - furled;
4. Hun - ger for pow - er, thirst to suc - ceed
5. Bless - ed are those who strug - gle for peace,

let them take hold in deeds full of light.
stock - piles but lead to ter - ror and fright.
let bombs be changed to bread for the world.
lead us a - way from peo - ple in need.
work - ing in hope that wars soon will cease.

Refrain

Je - sus still lives, a new hope to bring; then lay fear a - side and

with him come, sing: Ho - ly, ho - ly, ho - ly Im - mor - tal One.

66   O Zion, haste

Mary A. Thomson, 1894

James Walch, 1875

1. O   Zi - on,   haste,   thy   mis - sion high   ful - fill - ing,
2. Be - hold how   man - y   thou-sands still   are   ly - ing
3. Pro - claim to   ev - ery   peo -ple, tongue, and   na - tion
4. Give   of thine   own   to   bear   the   mes - sage glo - rious;

to   tell   to   all   the   world that   God   is   light,
bound   in   the   dark - some   pris - on - house of   sin,
that   God,   in   whom   they   live   and move, is   love;
give   of   thy   wealth   to   speed them   on   their   way;

that   he   who made   all   na - tions is   not   will - ing
with   none   to   tell   them   of   the   Sav - ior's   dy - ing,
tell   how   he stooped   to   save   his   lost cre - a - tion,
pour   out   thy   soul   for   them   in   prayer vic - to - rious;

one   soul should per - ish,   lost   in   shades of   night.
or   of   the   life   he   died   for   them   to   win.
and   died   on   earth   that   we   might live   a - bove.
O   Zi - on,   haste   to   bring the bright - er   day.

Refrain

Pub - lish glad tid - ings, tid - ings of peace;

tid - ings of Je - sus, re - demp - tion and re - lease.

Where cross the crowded ways **67**

Frank Mason North, 1903   *Sacred Melodies*, 1815

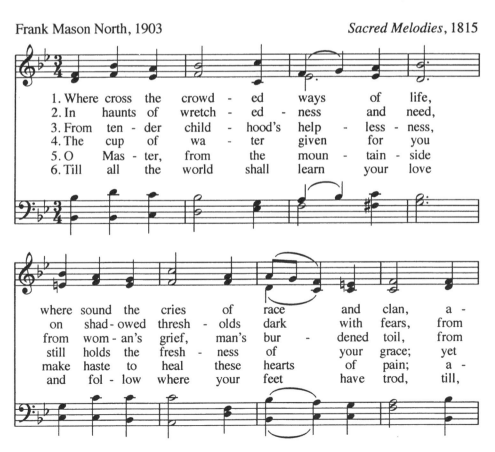

1. Where cross the crowd - ed ways of life,
2. In haunts of wretch - ed - ness and need,
3. From ten - der child - hood's help - less - ness,
4. The cup of wa - ter given for you
5. O Mas - ter, from the moun - tain - side
6. Till all the world shall learn your love

where sound the cries of race and clan, a -
on shad - owed thresh - olds dark with fears, from
from wom - an's grief, man's bur - dened toil, from
still holds the fresh - ness of your grace; yet
make haste to heal these hearts of pain; a -
and fol - low where your feet have trod, till,

bove the noise of self - ish strife, we
paths where hide the lures of greed, we
fam - ished souls, from sor - row's stress, your
long these mul - ti - tudes to view the
mong these rest - less throngs a - bide; O
glo - rious from your heaven a - bove, shall

hear your voice, O Son of man.
catch the vi - sion of your tears.
heart has nev - er known re - coil.
sweet com - pas - sion of your face.
tread the cit - y's streets a - gain.
come the cit - y of our God!

68 Send your Word

Yasushige Imakoma, 1965
trans., Nobuaki Hanaoka, 1983

Shozo Koyama, 1965

1. Send your Word, O Lord, like the rain, fall - ing down up -
2. Send your Word, O Lord, like the wind, blow - ing down up -
3. Send your Word, O Lord, like the dew, com - ing gent - ly up

on the earth. Send your Word. We seek your end - less
on the earth. Send your Word. We seek your won - drous
on the hills. Send your Word. We seek your end - less

grace, with souls that hun - ger and thirst, sor - row and
power, pure - ness that re - jects all sins, though they per -
love. For life that suf - fers in strife with ad - ver - si -

ag - o - nize. We would all be lost in
sist and cling. Bring us to com - plete vic -
ties and hurts, send your heal - ing power of

dark with - out your guid - ing light.
tory; set us all free in - deed.
love; we long for your new world.

69 God of change and glory
Many gifts, one Spirit

words and music, Al Carmines, 1973

1. God of change and glo - ry, God of time and space,
2. God of man - y col - ors, God of man - y signs,
3. Fresh - ness of the morn - ing, new - ness of each night,

when we fear the fu - ture, give to us your grace.
you have made us dif - ferent, bless - ing man - y kinds.
you are still cre - at - ing end - less love and light.

In the midst of chang - ing ways give us still the grace to
As the old ways dis - ap - pear, let your love cast out our
This we see, as shad - ows part, man - y gifts from one great

For the Giv-er, for the gifts, praise, praise, praise! *8va*

70   Rescue the perishing

Fanny J. Crosby, 1869   William H. Doane, 1870

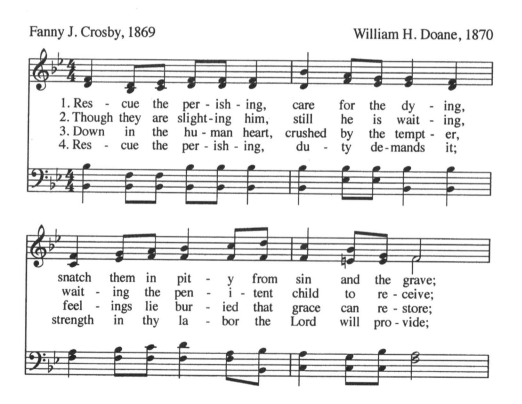

1. Res - cue the per - ish - ing, care for the dy - ing,
2. Though they are slight-ing him, still he is wait - ing,
3. Down in the hu - man heart, crushed by the tempt - er,
4. Res - cue the per - ish - ing, du - ty de-mands it;

snatch them in pit - y from sin and the grave;
wait - ing the pen - i - tent child to re - ceive;
feel - ings lie bur - ied that grace can re - store;
strength in thy la - bor the Lord will pro - vide;

weep o'er the err - ing one, lift up the fall - en,
plead with them ear - nest - ly, plead with them gent - ly;
touched by a lov - ing heart, wak - ened by kind - ness,
back to the nar - row way pa - tient - ly win them;

tell them of Je - sus, the might - y to save.
he will for - give if they on - ly be - lieve.
chords that were bro - ken will vi - brate once more.
tell the poor wan - derer a Sav - ior has died.

Refrain

Res - cue the per - ish-ing, care for the dy - ing;

Je - sus is mer - ci - ful, Je - sus will save.

71

Zhi ran fu yu hua tu shi
Lord, for thy revealing gifts

Ernest Y L. Yano, 1933
Mandarin translit., David C. Wu, 2006

ancient Chinese lute melody

Mandarin translit.: Zhi ran fu yu hua tu shi,
Na - ture is full of col - - or

Ling xin hua kai shi ren bi,
flow - 'ring from the ar - tis - - tic heart,

Tian jen liu lu yeh ying zhong,
na - ture gives a mus - ic sweet

Shen qi shi chian jian xing yi shu,
that re - veals a Fa - - ther's art.

Jing ying can dan shi jiu en,
He with care con - trives them all,

wan xiang ying ren jian jen shi. A - men.
thus per - ceived we know in part. A - men.

Lord, your church on earth 72

Hugh Sherlock, 1981   Joy Brown, 1981

1. Lord, your church on earth is seek - ing your re -
2. Free - dom give to those in bond - age, lift the
3. In the slums of ev - ery cit - y where the

new - al from a - bove. Teach us all the
bur - dens caused by sin; give new hope, new
bruised and lone - ly dwell, we shall show the

art of speak - ing with the ac - cent of your
strength, and cour - age, grant re - lease from fears with -
Sav - ior's pit - y, we shall of his mer - cy

love. We would heed your great com - mis - sion:
in. Light for dark - ness, joy for sor - row;
tell. In all lands and with all rac - es

Go you in - to ev - ry place, preach, bap - tize, ful -
love for ha - tred; peace for strife; these and count - less
we shall serve, and seek to bring hu - man - kind to

fill my mis - sion, serve with love and share my grace.
bless - ings fol - low as the Spir - it gives new life.
rend - er prais - es Christ to thee, Re - deem - er, King.

73 Your duty let the apostle show

Charles Wesley   Timothy E. Kimbrough, 1996

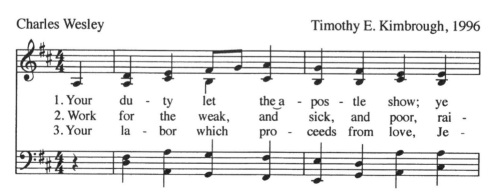

1. Your du - ty let the a - pos - tle show; ye
2. Work for the weak, and sick, and poor, rai -
3. Your la - bor which pro - ceeds from love, Je -

ought, ye ought to la - bor so, in
ment and food for them pro - cure, and
sus shall gra - cious - ly ap - prove, with

Je - sus' cause em - ployed, your call - ing's works at
mind - ful of God's Word, en - joy the bless - ed -
full fe - lic - i - ty, with bright est crowns your

times pur - sue, and keep the a - pos - tle
ness to give, lay out your get - tings
loan re - pay, and tell you in that

Paul in view, and use your hands for God.
to re - lieve the mem - bers of your Lord.
joy - ful day, "Ye did it un - to Me"

74 We've a story to tell to the nations

words and music, H. Ernest Nichol, 1896

1. We've a sto - ry to tell to the na - tions,
2. We've a song to be sung to the na - tions,
3. We've a mes - sage to give to the na - tions,
4. We've a Sav - ior to show to the na - tions,

that shall turn their hearts to the right, a
that shall lift their hearts to the Lord, a
that the Lord who reign - eth a - bove hath
who the path of sor - row hath trod, that

sto - ry of truth and mer - cy, a sto - ry of
song that shall con - quer e - vil and shat - ter the
sent us his Son to save us, and show us that
all of the world's great peo - ples might come to the

peace and light, a sto - ry of peace and light.
spear and sword, and shat - ter the spear and sword.
God is love, and show us that God is love.
truth of God, might come to the truth of God.

Refrain

For the dark - ness shall turn to dawn - ing, and the

dawn - ing to noon - day bright; and Christ's great king - dom shall

come on earth, the king - dom of love and light.

75 Child of joy and peace

Hunger Carol

Shirley Erena Murray, 1992   I-to Loh, 1996

1. Child of joy and peace born to ev - 'ry race— by your star, the wise will know you, East and
2. Born a - mong the poor on a sta - ble floor, you know our hung - er, weep our
3. Ev - 'ry child needs bread till the world is fed: your hands en - a - ble, all to
4. Son of pov - er - ty shame us till we see self - con - cerned, how we de - ny you, by our

76 In mission together

words and music, S T Kimbrough, Jr., 2004

refrain and arr.,
Jorge Lockward, 2004

1. We come from the moun - tains, the val - leys and
2. Though diff' - rent in cul - ture and modes of our
3. In Christ we're u - nit - ed, all bar - ri - ers

plains, the cit - ies and farm - lands a -
dress, tho' strange seems our lan - guage we
fall; there's no fav - ored gen - der, one

wait - ing the rains. Our cul - tures are
bold - ly con - fess that we are u -
fam' - ly for all: op - pressed, rich, and

man - y, our tongues ev - en more; our
nit - ed: one peo - ple, one voice. We're
need - y, the weak and the strong one

voic - es we raise to God our Cre - a - tor in glo - ri - ous praise.

77   Souls in heathen darkness

Cecil F. Alexander, 1852, 1859   Walter Bond Gilbert

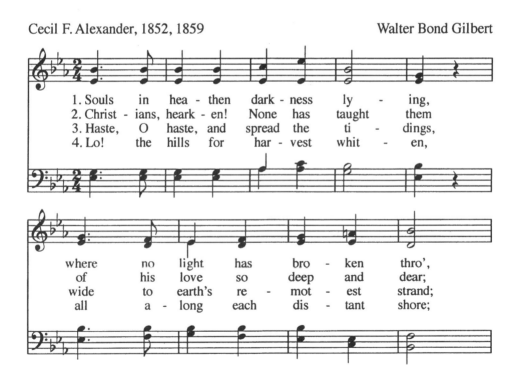

1. Souls   in   hea - then   dark - ness   ly -   ing,
2. Christ - ians, heark - en! None has   taught   them
3. Haste,   O   haste, and   spread   the   ti -   dings,
4. Lo!   the   hills   for   har - vest   whit -   en,

where   no   light   has   bro -   ken   thro',
of   his   love   so   deep   and   dear;
wide   to   earth's   re -   mot -   est   strand;
all   a - long   each   dis -   tant   shore;

INDEX OF NAMES

INDEX OF FIRST LINES AND COMMON TITLES

Introduction

This guide is to assist study leaders in the facilitation of the spiritual growth study on music and mission, *God's Mission, God's Song.* The purpose of the study is: 1) to gain an understanding of the role of music in the mission of the church; 2) to analyze and study mission hymns regarding their biblical and theological understanding of mission; 3) to determine, if possible, the relationship between mission hymns and the missionary movement; and 4) to expand our understanding of, and participation in, God's mission through the use of global song.

Brian Wren has described a hymn as "a poem, designed for group singing, and written as a sequence of identical units, called stanzas…. It can develop a theme, reach a conclusion, expound a doctrine, paraphrase scripture, or tell a story."[1] The Hebrew people were hymn singers and dancers. They sang of God's triumph over Pharaoh and other military victories. They sang the Psalms in worship and prayer, and vocalized their unhappiness and misery with the Psalms of lament. Hymns have been used for evangelism, mission, worship, and proclamation of the gospel since the early church. Paul wrote in Colossians 3:16: "Let the word of Christ dwell in you richly; teach and admonish one another in all wisdom; and with gratitude in your hearts sing psalms, hymns, and spiritual songs to God." Mary's Magnificat (Luke 1:46-55) is one of the most powerful and beautiful hymns recorded in the Scriptures.

It was during the eighteenth century that hymn singing became an acceptable expression of the Christian faith and was first used in worship. It was only natural then that mission hymns would be written and used in the modern missionary movement which started near the end of that century. Mission hymns continue to be an important part of the hymnody of the church as a means of telling the story of mission, inspiring giving to mission, proclaiming the theology of mission, and issuing God's call to missionary service.

Your Own Preparation as Leader

Some of you may already be saying: "I am not a singer or musician. How can I lead a group in a study of music and mission?" Do not be fainthearted! Musical ability is not necessary to lead this study. An appreciation of music and hymnody is desirable, but even this can be learned as you proceed in your preparation for leading.

1. Be spiritually prepared. Pray about the study. Use the text and hymns as a prayer book. Open your heart to God's guidance. Peruse the Scriptures with special attention to those mentioned in the text. Talk to a spiritual mentor or a spiritual director about your role as study leader and your thoughts and concerns about the study.

2. Read and reread the text and songs as often as necessary. Not only are you reading prose, but you are reading and studying poetry as well. Poetry generates a variety of meanings depending on the setting, the mood, and individual perspectives. Always ask yourself the question: "What does this hymn mean for the church today?" Your answer will not always be the same, nor will it be the same as the answers from others within your class. Be open to the Spirit as you reflect on the significance of the hymns for God's mission today.

3. If possible, sing or have someone sing for you the hymns in the text. Music also conveys an understanding of the lyrics of a hymn and may bring new significance to a hymn. A different tune for a hymn can change its meaning.

4. Listen to the CD that accompanies this study. Perhaps you can also find other recordings of some of the hymns not included on the CD. You might make an audiotape of a friend or yourself singing some of the hymns to use in the study.

5. Read and study as many of the books and resources included in the bibliography as you can locate. Check your town or city library, the church library, and the internet. Special attention should be

given to books dealing with the theology of mission and any writings regarding music and mission.

6. Note carefully the purposes of the study and the objective of each session. These are your goals as you lead the study.

7. Always be prepared. Preparation can reduce your stress level, help you project an attitude of learning and hospitality, and make the study a spiritual experience for yourself and the class.

Planning the Study

1. Plan the entire study. This guide is written for four two-hour sessions. You may have less or more time, so choose those activities and learning opportunities appropriate to your group and the time available. Make yourself a lesson plan including approximate times for each activity. Be as specific as necessary for your own comfort level. You might want to give to each participant the purposes of the study, a brief outline and objectives of each session, and the assignments for each session.

2. Make worship an integral part of the study. Hymns can be used as prayers, moments of praise, calls for mercy, laments, or opportunities for commitment. Be creative in your worship experiences and be open to the Spirit throughout each session. God may surprise you with an epiphany!

3. Look carefully at the space you will be using. Hopefully you can meet in a room with movable chairs, perhaps several tables, chalkboard or newsprint, and room for the musical or audiovisual equipment you intend to use. Make the space as comfortable as possible and allow room for movement and small group activity. If you are meeting in a sanctuary, auditorium, or another room with fixed furniture, try to make the space conducive to study. Perhaps colored scarves, small banners, or a variety of musical instruments, can provide focal points and change the atmosphere of the area.

4. Make the space an environment of learning. Posters, quotations, hymn phrases, etc. can be placed around the room. Mount them on construction paper to add color to the room and display as allowed by the facility. A table of books and other resources related to the study might be prepared. A display of old hymnals can also be fun and an interesting focal point. Be sure to have a CD player, a tape recorder, a piano, or other musical instruments (keyboard, recorder, etc.) that you intend to use available for all sessions. If the room is large a loudspeaker system might be needed. You also will want to have an overhead projector available for any transparencies you make for the study.

5. Gather all supplies ahead of time. This might include paper, pencils, pens, crayons, newsprint, chalk, etc. If you are copying materials be sure to observe all copyright rules and regulations. (Hymns that are under copyright can be used in a class setting and then collected afterwards, or projected via an overhead projector.)

6. Pay attention to the comfort of the participants. Try to provide sufficient lighting, adequate climate control, and access to restrooms. Either allow participants to leave the room as necessary or provide break time in every session. Vary activity so that there is movement within the room and conversations take place in different groupings. Enter into a covenant with the class that includes confidentiality in the class setting; that welcomes discussion and even disagreement; and agrees that at all times persons will be polite and accepting of each other.

7. Encourage the preparation of the participants. Each participant should have the text and a Bible for use in the classroom. Most will also want something for note-taking and other assignments. Encourage each person to participate in discussions, small group activities, and in the singing or reading of hymns. Also get volunteers to present parts of the worship experiences and give various reports. Underline the spiritual growth nature of this study and encourage all to be open to the Spirit in the midst of the class.

Timeline of Mission

Prepare a timeline of the "modern" missionary movement. Make it on newsprint or white paper table covering (comes in rolls) using various colors of heavy markers. Be sure to print clearly and large enough for the class to read it from a distance.

Denominational Organizations

1792	Baptist Missionary Society of England
1793	Sent William Carey as missionary to India
1810	American Board of Commissioners for Foreign Missions, Congregational
1812	Sent Adoniram and Ann Judson as missionaries to India
1813	Wesleyan Missionary Society, British Methodist Church
1819	Wyandot Indian Mission, Methodist Episcopal Church
1820	Missionary Society of the Methodist Episcopal Church
	Had sent missionaries to various locations in America for 20 years
1834	Board of Foreign Missions, Methodist Protestant Church
1839	Missionary Society of the Evangelical Association
1841	Home, Frontier, and Foreign Missionary Society, United Brethren Church
1880	Board of Home and Foreign Missions, Methodist Protestant Church
1939	Board of Missions, Methodist Church
1946	Board of Missions, Evangelical United Brethren Church
1968	General Board of Missions/Global Ministries, United Methodist Church

Women's Missionary Societies

1868   Woman's Foreign Missionary Society of
        New England, Congregational

1869   Woman's Foreign Missionary Society,
        Methodist Episcopal Church
                Sent Isabella Thoburn and Clara Swain
                as missionaries to India

1875   Women's Missionary Association,
        United Brethren Church

1878   Woman's Foreign Missionary Society,
        Methodist Episcopal Church South

1879   Woman's Foreign Missionary Society,
        Methodist Protestant Church

1880   Woman's Home Missionary Society,
        Methodist Episcopal Church

1884   Woman's Missionary Society,
        Evangelical Church

1890   Woman's Home Missionary Society,
        Methodist Episcopal Church, South

1893   Woman's Home Missionary Society,
        Methodist Protestant Church

1939   Woman's Society of Christian Service,
        Methodist Church

1946   Women's Society of World Service,
        Evangelical United Brethren Church

1973   United Methodist Women, United
        Methodist Church

Other Organizations and Movements

1770s-1860s   Various abolition and anti-slavery
               organizations formed

1830s-1900   Holiness movement active in Methodist
               Episcopal Church

1848   Seneca Falls Convention on
               Women's Rights

1858   YWCA came to US from England,
               where it was organized in 1855

1869   Woman's Christian Temperance Union

1869	National Woman Suffrage Association
1860s-1920s	Social gospel movement
1886	Student Volunteer Movement
1880-1930	Foreign missionary movement most active
1948	World Council of Churches
1950s and beyond	Mission seen and understood as God's mission, *missio Dei*

Continuing Drama

One possible way of building continuity into this study is to have three persons play the parts of Marjorie, Louise, and Pastor Janice throughout the study. The actresses can develop a miniature drama in their own words using dialogue ideas gleaned from the journey of the three as told in each chapter. Improvisation is essential to make this a fun and learning activity. A suggested outline of such a drama is:

> For Session 1 use the materials about the women found in Chapter 1.
>
> For the beginning of Session 2 use the materials in Chapter 2. Between Activities #2 and #3 use the materials in Chapter 3.
>
> For the opening of Session 3 use the materials at the beginning of Chapter 4. After Activity #2 use the material at the beginning of Chapter 5.
>
> For the opening of Session 4 use the materials at the end of Chapter 5 and the beginning of Chapter 6. The material near the end of Chapter 6 should be used just prior to the Service of Commitment.

Hymn Sings or Listening Time

As people gather for class you might want to have "hymn sings" of both familiar and unknown hymns used in the text. A pianist and possibly a song leader will be needed to learn the new hymns. Or you might have a listening time set up for people to learn some of the new hymns that are on the CD.

Purpose

• To explore biblical, theological, and Wesleyan understandings of mission and how they are expressed in mission hymns.

Preparation

1. Have the timeline ready and posted for the session. It should remain up throughout the study.

2. Place around the room the following quotations from hymns for Activity #1:

> "To tell to all the world that God is light."
> — Mary A. Thomson
>
> "Inspire our ways of learning through earnest,
> fervent prayer."
> — Leon M. Adkins
>
> "Tell the world what God has done."
> — Brian Wren
>
> "To care for all, without reserve, and spread his
> liberating word."
> — Fred Pratt Green
>
> "Work for the weak, and sick, and poor."
> — Charles Wesley

3. Have a few Bibles for those who did not bring their own. Have all Bible references, hymn numbers, and discussion questions on a single handout for Activity #3. Give all assignments to everyone, making reporting easier. This is also helpful for those who intend to lead the study in another setting.

4. Activity #4 is a group discussion. Prepare yourself by having a good understanding of the definitions of mission given in the text. Supplement that material with other resources you have read and the two quotations included in this guide. This activity attempts to move the group toward the understanding that the mission is God's and we are participants in God's mission.

5. Make a banner to hang in front of the room that says "God's mission
- *missio Dei.*"

Opening Worship

Hymn:		"O Zion, Haste" (#66) stanzas 1 and 2
Scripture:		Isaiah 40:9-11, John 8:12
Hymn:		"O Zion, Haste" stanza 3
Scripture:		Matthew 28:18-20
Litany:		
	Right:	Give of thine own to bear the message glorious,
	Left:	give of thy wealth to speed them on their way;
	Right:	pour out thy soul for them in prayer victorious,
	Left:	O Zion, haste to bring the brighter day.
Hymn Response:		"O Zion, Haste" chorus
Prayer:		Dear God: We have heard that you are light and love. May we be open to share that message with the world in ways that help to bring about the reign of God. Amen

Learning Activities

Activity #1:

Ask the participants to stand in front of one of the posted hymn
quotations that best describes their understanding of mission and
discuss with each other the following questions. One person should
take notes on the discussion so that a brief report can be given.
Introductions should be made within the groups if everyone does not
know each other.

> What does this phrase say about mission?
> How can this type of mission be conducted in today's world?
> In a simple phrase or a single word complete the sentence:
> "Mission is....."

Reports can be given after about five minutes of discussion. As leader, note the similarities and differences in the responses. Also make a list on newsprint of the words or phrases that complete the sentence: "Mission is...." Keep this list for use in Activity #4.

Activity #2:

Share briefly the story behind the hymn "O Zion, Haste" and discuss the analysis of the hymn found on pages 2-3. Emphasize the ordinary life of the writer, her commitment to mission, and her challenge to give and pray for mission. Use this as an illustration of the purposes of the study as stated in the opening paragraph of this guide.

Activity #3:

Divide into small groups, making sure that within each group there is at least one Bible. One person should serve as reporter. Ask each group to read aloud the scriptural references and the hymn and then spend a moment in silent meditation. The questions and comments should then be discussed. This whole process will take 15 to 20 minutes.

Group 1: Micah 6:6-8
"What Does the Lord Require" (#47)
To whom is this hymn addressed?
How do you feel about the questions in the hymn?
In what way has the hymn writer expanded your understanding of the biblical reference and mission?

Group 2: Matthew 28:18-20
"Go, Make of All Disciples" (#10)
How does the hymn writer describe and define discipleship?
What are the goals of mission described in this hymn?
Paraphrase stanza three in your own words.

Group 3:   Luke 24:49, Acts 1:8, and Luke 4:16-21

"There's a Spirit in the Air" (#43)

What is the role of the Holy Spirit
in mission as stated in these passages
and this hymn?

What personal message does the hymn
have for participants in mission?

How do you interpret the phrase:
"Live tomorrow's life today!"

Group 4:   John 20:19-23

"The Church of Christ, in Every Age" (#41)

What is the relationship between the
risen Christ and the church in mission
described in the hymn?

What do you see to be the servant role
of followers of Christ?

Paraphrase stanza five in your own words.

Group 5:   Ephesians 4:1-16

"We All Are One in Mission" (#3)

What are the similarities and differences
between the Scripture passage and
the hymn?

What is a call to mission? Do you receive
it only once? Identify your call.

What is the goal of mission as defined in
this hymn?

Group 6:   Luke 10:1-20

"Lord of the Harvest, Hear" (page 8)

How does this hymn of Charles
Wesley repeat John Wesley's
"Works of Mercy" found on pages 7-8?

To whom is this hymn addressed?
What type of hymn is it?

What is the task of the workers as
described in the hymn?

When it appears that most groups have finished discussing, call the groups back together with the singing of "There's a Spirit in the Air" (#43). Have each group share their findings and perhaps lead the class in singing or reading several stanzas of their hymn.

Activity #4

Building upon the early responses of the group to the completion of the sentence: "Mission is...," the biblical references and hymns used in the previous activity, and your own additional thoughts or comments, have a group discussion that centers on the concept that the mission is God's mission *(missio Dei)*. For the latter, carefully study the quotations below as well as the definitions in the text on pages 9 and 10. Key thoughts might be:

* Love is the motivation for mission — God's love for us and our love for others.
* It is God's mission, not the church's mission nor is the mission ours.
* Through mission we participate in God's work in the world.
* Mission is not our work, but the work of the Spirit.
* Discipleship is the goal — turning to God and to the neighbor.

Discuss with the group the hymns they feel express this theology.

Additional quotations:

> Our mission has no life of its own: only in the hands of the sending God can it truly be called mission, not least since the missionary initiative comes from God alone....In the new image mission is not primarily an activity of the church, but an attribute of God. God is a missionary God. Mission is thereby seen as a movement from God to the world; the church is viewed as an instrument for that mission. There is church because there is mission, not vice versa. To participate in mission is to participate in the movement of God's love toward people, since God is a fountain of sending love.[2]

Our missionary activities are only authentic insofar as they reflect participation in the mission of God. The primary purpose of the church in mission can therefore not simply be the planting of churches or the saving of souls; rather, it has to be service to the *missio Dei*, representing God in and over against the world, pointing to God, holding up the God-child before the eyes of the world in a ceaseless celebration of the Feast of the Epiphany....The *missio Dei* is God's activity, which embraces both the church and the world, and in which the church may be privileged to participate.[3]

Closing Centering

Have the group read silently the hymn, "Sois la Semilla" ("You Are the Seed") (#31). Then ask for popcorn responses to this question: "How can I participate in God's mission according to this hymn?" Close with three people reading the verses of the hymn and all singing the chorus after each verse. As leader, close by reading the chorus as a prayer.

Assignments for the Entire Study

1. Ask each person to choose one hymn from the text or hymn section for reflection and meditation during the course of the study. The reflections can be recorded in a journal and might include paraphrases of the stanzas of the hymn, scriptural references reflected in the hymn, the theology of mission articulated in the hymn, and its impact on their involvement in God's mission.

2. Encourage everyone who desires to write a mission hymn. They might choose to set it to a particular familiar tune, to write a new tune, or to write only a text. Time for sharing of these new hymns will be included in the last session.

3. If there is someone within the class who does interpretative dance, ask them to prepare an interpretative dance of "Here I Am, Lord" (#34) for Session 3.

Assignments for Session 2

1. Each participant should read Chapters 1-3 and the hymns included in those chapters.

2. Have two persons prepare a report about the early missionary societies and their hymns using the material found on pages 12 to 17 of the text. Hymns discussed should include:

"Jesus Shall Reign"
"Behold the Heathen Waits to Know"
"Great God! The Nations of the Earth"
"Souls in Heathen Darkness Lying"

3. Ask someone to give a five-minute report on the children's mission hymns as found on page 28 in Chapter 3 and "Jesus Belongs to All Children" (#17). If the person knows of other mission hymns for children, encourage sharing those as well.

4. Ask someone to give a five-minute report on the two hymns, "The Coming of the King" and "The Woman's Hymn." These hymns give unique perspectives on mission from a woman's viewpoint. Include in the report something about both writers.

---

[1] Brian Wren, *Praying Twice* (Louisville, Ky.: Westminster John Knox Press, 2000), 100-101.
[2] David J. Bosch, *Transforming Mission* (Maryknoll, N.Y.: Orbis Books, 1991), 390.
[3] Ibid., 391.

Purposes

- To explore the development and changes in theology of mission in mission hymns.
- To discover the influence of various religious and social movements on the missionary movement and its hymns.

Preparation

1. Make sure the timeline is still posted. It will be needed in several of the activities in this session.

2. Ask five or six persons to do the responsive prayer during the opening worship. Have it printed out for them if all of them do not have the guide. Also involve several people in the closing worship experience.

3. Set up a CD player and have it ready for use in Activity #3.

4. Prepare your presentation for Activity #2, the discussions in Activities #1, #3, and #7, and make sure that all reports are ready.

Opening Worship

Call to Worship:	Great God! The nations of the earth
	Are by creation thine;
	And in thy works, by all beheld,
	Thy power and glory shine.
Hymn:	"Jesus Shall Reign" (#18)
Scripture:	Matthew 28:16-20
Responsive Prayer:	
One Voice:	Lord, speak to me, that I may speak in living echoes of your tone.
Several Voices:	Let us seek your erring children lost and lone.
One Voice:	O teach me, Lord, that I may teach the precious things you impart.

Several Voices:	May our words reach the hidden depths of many a heart.
One Voice:	O fill me Lord and use even me, just as you will, and when, and where.
Several Voices:	Let us show your praise and tell your love until we share your rest and joy. Amen

Learning Activities

Activity #1

Have the report given regarding the early missionary societies and their hymns as assigned in the previous session. Lead a group discussion after the report centered on the following questions and comments.

What do you feel was the basic theological motivation for the early missionary work? How did Watts's hymn, "Jesus Shall Reign" encourage this activity?

The word "heathen" was often used. What is your understanding of the meaning of the word? What are your reactions to this word? Is there another word that you would find appropriate for today?

When "light" and "darkness" are used to describe those touched by Jesus and those who are not, what is your reaction? Is not God in the darkness? (For further work on God and darkness see Isaiah 45:3 and Psalm 19:1-2 and consider the significance of darkness or night at the time of the birth, the death, and resurrection of Jesus.) What words would you use today?

What is the main point of Cecil Alexander's hymn, "Souls in Heathen Darkness Lying"? How would you state it in today's terms and language?

Activity #2

Move directly into a brief presentation about the shifts in mission theology that took place in the beginning of the nineteenth century.

Illustrate with the hymns mentioned in the text including "Over the Ocean Wave" and "From Greenland's Icy Mountains." Deal with some or all of these questions:

> Was the gospel distorted by the missionary societies?
> Did the hymns initiate or reflect this theology?
> Consider the implication that darkness implied sin.
> What is the connection to racism then and now?

Determine as a group if there is still some of this mission theology alive in the world today. Close this activity with a discussion of "Assembled at Thy Great Command" as found on page 19, noting the theology expressed in this hymn.

Activity #3

Listen to the segment on the CD entitled "Visions of Justice." This is a segment approximately ten minutes long that highlights hymns and songs of justice. As the group listens have them note the justice issue addressed in each song. Supplement the CD with a review of the abolition and temperance hymns included in the text.

Lead the group in a discussion of the holiness and social gospel movements and their impact on mission activity. Give special attention to the appeal of holiness to women; the quotation by Leonard Sweet (page 23); reform movements within society; and the appeal of the social gospel. Use the timeline as appropriate.

An optional addition to this activity is to discuss the current justice hymns included in Chapter 5 at this point. (This same activity is suggested in Session 3, so decide carefully if you also wish to deal with the justice hymns in this session.) Divide into four groups, with each group assigned one of the justice issues: peace, children, environment, or poverty. Have the groups discuss their emotional reactions to the hymns. Deal with questions such as: How does the hymn inspire you to action? Where can this hymn be used and what will be its impact? Is the hymn controversial?

Activity #4

Missionary societies became very important after the Civil War. The hymns that were used in these organizations molded mission theology for the period prior to World War I. Divide into five groups with each group assigned one of the following hymns:

"Christ for the World We Sing"
"Rescue the Perishing"
"We've a Story to Tell to the Nations"
"Where Cross the Crowded Ways of Life"
"Heralds of Christ"

Ask the groups to read and study the hymn, read the materials in the text about the hymn, and then determine and analyze the understanding of mission as stated in the hymn. Each group should be prepared to give a brief report. The analysis should include such things as:

* Main theme of the hymn
* Key words used and their meaning or symbolism
* Biblical references that could be cited for the hymn
* Basic theology articulated in the hymn
* Problems or concerns that the hymn raises for your group

This activity could close with the singing of at least one stanza or the chorus of each of the hymns.

Activity #5

Have a five-minute report of children's songs about mission. This was an advance assignment made at the last session.

Activity #6

Have a five-minute report of the two hymns, "The Coming of the King" and "The Woman's Hymn." Emphasis should be on the feminist understandings of mission in both hymns. This was an advance assignment made at the last session. Group reactions to these hymns might raise some questions or comments about the unique understanding women may have regarding involvement in God's mission. Remember to note the dates when these hymns were written.

Activity #7

Do a comparison study of the four Assembly theme songs with the entire group. The hymns are:

"Come! Peace of God"
"Eternal God Whose Power Upholds"
"Many Gifts, One Spirit"
"Make Plain the Vision"

Sing the hymns noting rhythm, musical style, and the message of the words. Share reactions to the hymns in popcorn fashion. Do the hymns fit the stated theme of the Assembly? Would you leave the event singing the hymn? How can theme hymns impact mission, especially in an organization such as United Methodist Women?

Closing Centering

A responsive hymn reading of "Where Cross the Crowded Ways of Life":

Reader:	In the midst of the noise of racial strife, greed, and the tears of poverty we hear the voice of Jesus.
Solo or Group:	Sing stanzas 1 and 2 of the hymn.
Reader:	Christ is present in the world and has a special affinity for the poor.
Solo or Group:	Read stanzas 3 and 4 of the hymn.
Reader:	Come, Jesus, into the city, into our community, and into our hearts. May we be your grace and serve your children with love and justice.
Group:	Sing stanzas 5 and 6 of the hymn.
Prayer:	Intercessory prayer for those living in poverty in our community.

Assignments for Session 3

1. Each participant should read Chapters 4 and 5 and the hymns included in those chapters.

2. Have two people prepare a dialogue report of no more than 15 minutes regarding the materials in Chapter 4 under the headings of "Early Missionaries and Music," and "Ethnomusicology and Mission." Encourage them to emphasize the following:

   - Confusion and opposition of the early missionaries regarding indigenous music;
   - The work of Tom Colvin, Bliss Wiant, and T. Janet Surdam in bringing indigenous music into the church;
   - The story that Pablo Sosa tells, and the recent work of I-to Loh in Asia;
   - Summary of the role of translation, transplanted music, and indigenous hymns.

3. Have someone prepare a presentation on the section in Chapter 5 entitled "Mission Hymns Requiring a Personal Response." Emphasis should be placed on the diversity of God's call. Highlight the hymns "Brighten the Corner Where You Are" (#51), "Lord of All Nations, Grant Me Grace" (#19), "I'm Gonna Live So God Can Use Me" (#1), and "Help Us Accept Each Other" (#12). The report should be no more than 10 minutes in length and include the group singing of at least one of the hymns.

4. Ask someone to assume the role of Grace Noll Crowell and make a brief first person presentation to the class. Emphasis should be placed on her writing, her understanding of mission, and her involvement in the Woman's Division of Christian Service.

5. Remind the group to do their journal writing regarding their selected hymn. Encourage the writing of new mission hymns.

Purposes

- To explore the role of the missionary in the development of hymns used in a mission context.
- To gain an understanding of ethnomusicology and its role in religious music.
- To review some current justice hymns and discuss how they can be used today.
- To learn the thoughts of present-day missionaries about mission hymns.

Preparation

1. Post the definition of ethnomusicology as found on page 38 in the opening paragraph. This is needed for Activity #1.

2. Place around the room all of the comments by missionaries regarding the hallmarks of a good mission hymn as found on pages 56 to 57.

3. Make a list on newsprint of the 10 hymns that most often influenced the calling of persons to mission service as found on page 51. Post this so it can be used in Activity #3.

4. Ask people to take part in the worship experiences.

5. Have the CD player in place and any other equipment you intend to use.

Opening Worship

Celebrative Music: Play the hymn "Ye Servants of God." Have participants follow along in the text, (#46).

Voice from the Group:

Say, isn't this the old Charles Wesley hymn that is often used at ordinations or consecration services of missionaries? This is a much livelier tune and I LIKE IT!

Voice 2 from the Group:

> You are correct. This is Brother Charles and the music is that of Lim Swee Hong of Singapore. The words are given new meaning with this music and the hymn becomes a joyful hymn of praise and commitment. Wesley declares that we all are to proclaim the gospel to everyone and that the reign of God is everywhere. That's a good understanding of mission. The scriptural basis that Wesley used for this hymn is Revelation 7, not the usual mission text. Listen to the Scripture.

Scripture: Revelation 7:9-12

Reader:

> To proclaim the gospel is to preach, to teach, to heal, to praise, to advocate for justice, to show mercy, to love, to offer Jesus to all, to tell of God's work in the world.... To proclaim the gospel is to be a disciple of Jesus in all that we do and all that we are. Some of us have received or will receive a call to specialized service within the church, while all of us receive daily a call to be participants in God's mission. Let us be alert to our call. LISTEN! LISTEN! God is calling each of us. Let us spend a few moments in silent prayer listening to God and praying for God's guidance.

Silent Prayer, followed by the English translation of the French hymn "Soutiens Ma Foi" as found on page 55.

> Christ is the peace looked for
> by my soul,
> O Lord increase my faith.
> Take me Lord as I am
> God of Jacob increase my faith.

Hymn: "Ye Servants of God" (#46). You may choose to play the CD again, sing along

with the CD, or sing the hymn as a group
with piano or keyboard.

Learning Activities
Activity #1

Have the dialogue report presented regarding "Early Missionaries
and Music" and "Ethnomusicology and Mission." Call attention to the
definition of ethnomusicology as posted. Don't let the presentation go
over 20 minutes. Be prepared to pick up on any essentials you feel
were omitted from the report.

End the report by singing Tom Colvin's hymn from Malawi, "Come,
Let Us Seek Our God's Protection" (#63) using a leader-response style
as indicated in the text. Follow this with "Jesus Christ Sets Free to
Serve" (#5) by I-to Loh. Be sure that the group understands that both
these authors were missionaries and worked to see that indigenous
music was used in worship.

Activity #2

Have each participant answer the following questions and then discuss
their answers in groups of two or three.

> What is your favorite hymn? Why?
> What two hymns have nurtured and sustained you?
> How and when?
> What hymn has influenced your calling to be a disciple
> of Jesus?

After a brief time for discussion get popcorn feedback from the entire
group. Use this discussion as a lead into the discussion of similar
questions that were asked of active and retired missionaries. Refer to
the section in the text about hymns that nurtured and sustained the
missionaries. Tell Dorothy Gilbert's story as found on page 54 as well
as Marion Muthiah's comment on "Great Is Thy Faithfulness." Or
ask someone to be Dorothy Gilbert and read or tell her story and ask
someone to read Marion Muthiah's comment.

Activity #3

Have the report given regarding God's call and hymns that require a personal response as assigned in the last session. Emphasis here is placed on God's call to discipleship for all believers.

Review the posted list of hymns that influenced the calling to mission service of the surveyed missionaries. Compare that with the group responses to the same question in Activity #2 and the hymns discussed in the report. Look carefully at "I'll Go Where You Want Me to Go" (#28) and "The Voice of God Is Calling" on page 52. Give special attention to the mission theology and the understanding of God's call in each.

Would these hymns appeal to young people today? What is a good hymn to call people to participate in God's mission today? Call attention to the hallmarks of a good mission hymn as stated by the missionaries. Use these hallmarks to determine the validity of the hymns of calling noted by the missionaries, the group, and in the report.

If someone has prepared an interpretative dance of "Here I Am, Lord," have the dance performed to close this activity.

Activity #4

Have a time of personal reflection using the African-American spiritual "I'm Gonna Live So God Can Use Me" (#1). The hymn can be sung by the group or as a solo. Encourage the group to reflect on their own calling.

Activity #5

A visit from Grace Noll Crowell. She will be talking about her theology of mission and some of her writings about mission. Introduce Mrs. Crowell using the materials found on pages 64 and 65.

Activity #6

Divide into four groups and assign one of the justice issues (peace, children, environment, and poverty) to each group. Have the groups read together the hymns regarding their issue and then discuss the following questions. Each group will be expected to report back and present either by singing, choral reading, or some other means one of their hymns.

> How does the hymn inspire you to action around the justice issue?
>
> Where can this hymn be used and what will be its impact?
>
> How does the hymn qualify as a good mission hymn?
>
> Is the hymn controversial? Will it cause controversy?
>
> How can this hymn be used to call people to involvement in justice advocacy?

Activity #7

An alternative way to deal with the contemporary justice hymns is to select one of the justice issues based on what you consider to be the priority in the world or your community. Divide into two or three groups with each group assigned a specific hymn from that issue. Each group is to create a five-minute worship service using only the hymn and a Scripture passage of their own choosing. The purpose of the worship is to enlist persons to advocate for the justice concern. The services may be used as the closing centering experience or shared at another moment in the class.

Closing Centering

Scripture:	Amos 5:23-24
Reflection:	The prophet Amos was tired of the noisy singing of the psalms of justice. He knew the people did not implement what they were singing. Jesus had to deal with the same thing as the leaders of the temple talked and sang about following the law of God, but did not show mercy and love to the people. Do we understand and believe that justice work is a requirement

of discipleship and involvement in God's mission? Are we avoiding God's call to work for justice in our world?

Hymn: "Tú has venido a la orilla" ("Lord, When You Came to the Seashore") (#54, #55)

Assignments for Session 4

1. Each participant should have read the entire text prior to the last session and studied all the hymns in the text and hymn section.

2. A panel of hymn writers will be part of the next session. Ask persons to assume the role of one of the following: Mary Oyer, Pablo Sosa, Brian Wren, Per Harling, Shirley Erena Murray, or I-to Loh. Each person should read carefully the materials in the text and the hymns in the hymn section written by their chosen writer. They should be prepared to speak in the first person. The leader will moderate the panel, introduce the panelists, and ask appropriate questions of each writer. Share the individual questions found in Activity #4 of Session 4 with each presenter of the hymn writer.

3. Remind the group of their journaling assignment and the writing of a mission hymn.

4. Ask two people to prepare a presentation of hymns from the following hymnals as discussed in the text: *Mil Voces Para Celebrar* (see page 58), *Come, Let Us Worship* (see page 59), *Mir Vam (Peace to You)* (see pages 82-83), and the Cambodian hymnal as discussed on page 83. One hymn from each hymnal will be sufficient. For the hymn from the Russian hymnal, "Nye khram, nye zolotoye zdanye," ("The Church of God Is Not a Temple") the class can follow the song in the hymn section while it is played on the CD.

SESSION 4

Purposes

- To engage in conversation with current hymn writers regarding mission hymns for today's congregations.
- To explore the concept of global religious music and the Global Praise Program of the General Board of Global Ministries.
- To commit to be advocates for the use of mission hymns in our local congregations.
- To renew our commitment to participate in God's mission.

Preparation

1. Singing and listening to music will be prominent in this session. You might want to have a keyboard or piano in the room and a pianist available if someone in the class is not willing to play. Also have the CD player ready for use.

2. As leader you will moderate the panel discussion of hymn writers described in Activity #4. Review carefully the questions for each writer and be prepared to do follow-up if necessary. Keep the panel lively and the class involved in singing or reading the hymns as suggested. Set up the room for a panel discussion using tables and chairs in the front or a row of chairs facing the group. If microphones are needed in the room, have more than one or a movable microphone that can be shared.

3. Determine at the beginning of the session if anyone has a new mission hymn to present. Allow time for these presentations, even if it means you omit several of the activities. This is an important part of the study and these hymns and the writers need to be honored.

4. Place around the room the hymn phrases found at the beginning of each of the chapters. Mount them on construction paper in an attractive manner. The phrases are:

"To tell to all the world that God is light."

— Mary A. Thomson

"Peoples and realms of every tongue dwell on his love with sweetest song."

— Isaac Watts

"The cup of water given for you still holds the freshness of your grace."

— Frank Mason North

"Jesus, Jesu, fill us with your love, show us how to serve the neighbors we have from you."

— Tom Colvin

"Break down the wall that would divide your children, Lord."

— Olive Wise Spannaus

"The church is meant for mission, giving glory to God's name."

— Ruth Duck

These phrases will be used in the opening worship.

5. Copy the litany in the opening worship experience for everyone.

6. Be prepared to put a simple worship center in place for the closing time of commitment. This might include a colored scarf on a table, an open Bible, a candle, or a cross. Also have index cards available for the entire group for use in the service.

Opening Worship

Centering music: Play from the CD the segment "Brich mit den Hungrigen dein Brot" ("Break with the hungry your own bread") (#60). Have the class follow along in the hymn section.

Litany

One Voice: Jesus spoke to them, saying, "I am the light of the world. Whoever follows me will never walk in darkness but will have the light of life" (John 8:12).

All Voices: As participants in God's mission we must "tell to all the world that God is light."

One Voice: "For God so loved the world that he gave his only Son, so that everyone who believes in him may not perish but may have eternal life" (John 3:16).

All Voices: "Peoples and realms of every tongue dwell on his love with sweetest song." May our songs and deeds reflect the love of God.

One Voice: "I was hungry and you gave me food, I was thirsty and you gave me something to drink" (Matthew 25:35).

All Voices: Thank you, God, that "the cup of water given for you still holds the freshness of your grace."

One Voice: "So if I, your Lord and Teacher, have washed your feet, you also ought to wash one another's feet. For I have set you an example, that you also should do as I have done to you" (John 13:14-15).

All Voices: "Jesu, Jesu, fill us with your love, show us how to serve the neighbors we have from you."

One Voice: "There is one body and one Spirit, just as you were called to the one hope of your calling, one Lord, one faith, one baptism, one God and Father of all, who is above all and through all and in all" (Ephesians 4:4-6).

All Voices: May you, O God, creator of all, help us "break down the wall that would divide your children, Lord." Give us strength and courage for this task.

One Voice: "You will receive power when the Holy Spirit has come upon you; and you will be my witnesses in Jerusalem, in all Judea and Samaria, and to the ends of the earth" (Acts 1:8).

All Voices: It is the Holy Spirit that enables mission and calls each of us and the church to participate in God's mission. "The church is meant for mission, giving glory to God's name." Thanks be to God!

Hymn:	"As a Fire Is Meant for Burning" (#58)
	Sing this hymn as a prayer, pausing after each stanza for a period of silent prayer.

Learning Activities

Activity #1

A presentation of hymns from the Russian, Cambodian, Spanish, and Korean-American hymnals should be given as assigned at the last session. This is to be a singing and listening presentation with talking limited to brief explanations of the hymnals. Encourage the class to try at least one of the hymns in the first language.

Activity #2

Each person was asked at the first session to do journaling around one mission hymn. In groups of three or four have the members share their insights. Feedback should center on the insights about mission that were gained from the hymns. Each group should share one paraphrase of a stanza that they feel is significant. Be sure to have the original stanza and hymn source shared as well.

Activity #3

Lead the group in a discussion of the understanding of global song as found on pages 78 to 82 and pages 84 to 85 regarding Youth Mission Chorales. Points to be highlighted include:

* A general understanding of globalization including the religious music industry.
* Definition of global song as understood by the Global Praise Program (page 80).
* Ways to honor the culture of another group by singing their songs.
* Analysis of the theology of mission expressed in the hymns used.
* Involvement of young people in evangelizing through music.

Introduce the hymns found in this section in a "hymn-sing" type style and/or listen to some of the hymns on the CD. Again try to sing part of the hymn in the original language. You may choose to intersperse the singing or listening with the verbal presentation suggested in the preceding paragraph. Use at least the following hymns:

"If Walking Is Our Vocation" (#33) - could be read
"Yarabba ssalami" ("O, God of peace") (#61) - sing together
"Nurtured by the Spirit" (#59) - sing along with CD
"Order My Steps" - listen to CD

Activity #4

A panel presentation of hymn writers. You will be the moderator. The questions and comments given below are to guide the discussion and are given as suggestions only. Be informal, but allow time and space for serious presentations by the writers and involvement of the entire group. Be creative in your role as moderator. Additional biographical materials can be found in the books listed in the bibliography or on the internet.

Mary K. Oyer

Introductory material: Born in 1923, Oyer is Professor Emerita of music at Goshen College and Elkhart Theological Seminary in Indiana. She is a church music specialist with extensive experience in international music, specializing in African music. She still leads workshops, conducts singing, and teaches as a visiting professor in Taiwan. Oyer is a Mennonite and has been a hymnbook editor in that denomination. She served on the hymnal committee for the most recent Mennonite hymnal of 1992.

Questions: How have your life experiences and world events influenced your feelings about mission hymns? What do you see to be the characteristics of a good mission hymn? What hymns do you feel are needed for today and why? (This question is geared to her concern about Kyries.) Sing the Kyries (#37-39) and then reflect on her comments in silence.

Pablo Sosa

Introductory material: Born in 1933, Sosa is a Methodist pastor and musician in Buenos Aires, Argentina. He writes both words and music for his hymns, teaches worship and liturgy at the Protestant Institute for Higher Education, and is a leader of global song in many international events. Sosa was the song leader for the 1990 Assembly of United Methodist Women in Kansas City. He is a member of the Global Praise Working Group.

Questions: What kind of global mission songs are needed today? Do you feel the song "Momento novo" ("In This New Moment") (#29) is a good mission hymn, and if so, why? Listen to this hymn on the CD with the group following along in their texts.

Per Harling
Introductory material: Born in 1948, Harling is a Lutheran minister from Sweden. He is a local church pastor, musician, and a writer of liturgy and worship materials. He was the editor of *Worshipping Ecumenically*, a worship resource of the World Council of Churches. Harling was one of the song leaders at the 2002 Assembly of United Methodist Women in Philadelphia. He writes music for children as well as for adults. He is a member of the Global Praise Working Group.

Questions: Please tell us about your hymn "Du är helig" ("You Are Holy") (#40). Why do you see it as a mission hymn? Ask the group to sing along with the CD version of this hymn.

Brian Wren
Introductory material: Brian Wren is an ordained minister in the British Congregational Church and was born in 1936. He is a teacher, author, and writer of hymns. Wren is now living and teaching in the United States.

Questions: Do you encourage local congregations to sing the mission hymns of other cultures and why?

Shirley Erena Murray
Introductory material: Born in 1931, Murray is a Presbyterian lay-woman from New Zealand. She started writing hymns when she was in her 50s and is an outstanding contemporary hymn writer. She was

brought up as a Methodist, but became Presbyterian when she married a Presbyterian clergyman. Murray has been a teacher of languages, active in Amnesty International, and is a recipient of the New Zealand Order of Merit.

Questions: What do you think makes a good mission hymn for today? How would you analyze your hymn "Every Day" (#53)? Sing the hymn or have it sung by a soloist.

I-to Loh
Introductory material: Loh, born in 1936, is a retired seminary president and teacher. He served for twelve years as a missionary of The United Methodist Church in the Philippines. He is an ethno-musicologist by training and profession and has done a great deal of work with Asian cultural music. He is a native of Taiwan and the editor of *Sound the Bamboo,* the hymnal of the Christian Conference of Asia. Loh is a member of the Global Praise Working Group.

Questions: Your setting of the poem by Shirley Murray, "Child of Joy and Peace," is unique. How did you come to write this music? What does the hymn say to you? The group should turn to the hymn (#75) as Dr. Loh talks about it. Have the pianist play the melody and then have the group sing the entire hymn.

Closing comments
Other contemporary hymn writers could not be with us. We are sorry that Nolan E. Williams, Jr., Sister Delores Dufner, and Carolyn Gillette are not with us. Let us honor their writing by singing together "Here Am I" (#42) as symbolic of all those who are writing from their hearts about God's mission.

Activity #5
Share with each other the new mission hymns that have been written by members of the class. Have the writers express their feelings about the hymn and their scriptural or theological motivations for the hymn.

Service of Commitment

Scripture:	Psalm 146
Hymn:	"The Spirit Sends Us Forth to Serve." (Words are on page 92 of the text and the tune LAND OF REST is Number 269 in *The United Methodist Hymnal.*)
Scripture:	Luke 4:16-21

Meditation in Dialogue

Reader One: Preparation is required for all who desire to participate in God's mission.

Reader Two: That means research and study, listening and dialoguing with a variety of people about justice issues, standing in solidarity with people who are fighting for equality, and being in touch with God on a daily basis.

Reader Three: Our spiritual preparation is also in our singing and perhaps even in the writing of hymns. It is in our singing that we are challenged to remember that the mission is God's and that God has given to the world the gift of grace. It is in our singing that we may become uncomfortable with God's call to involvement in mission.

Reader One: We must be imaginative in our approach to involvement in God's mission and be willing to imagine the newness God intends for our world.

Reader Two: We must be bold in word, deed, and song even if risk and danger is required.

Reader Three: Our singing must reflect our willingness to claim the Holy Spirit as a guide, comforter, and challenger to our involvement in mission.

Reader One:	God's mission demands faithfulness, a sense of fidelity to God, and a trust in God that we experience through Jesus, the Christ.
Reader Two:	It is faithfulness that lets us believe that "God is alive in our midst in hope and joyful solidarity." It is faithfulness that lets us "sing with the sorrowful a song."
Reader Three:	It is faithfulness that "keeps us fervent in our witness." It is faithfulness that causes each of us "to bind myself to peace, to make strife and envy cease."
Reader One:	As participants in God's mission we must sing both a doxology and a lament and sometimes at the same time.
Reader Two:	As participants in God's mission we must weep over the Jerusalems of today, sing the songs of our brothers and sisters around the world, and celebrate each sign of God's newness in our midst.
Reader Three:	As participants in God's mission our songs must be imaginative, bold, faithful, and full of God's love.
Commitment:	Ask each person to write on an index card their commitment to involvement in God's mission and how music is going to assist them. Also have them complete this sentence: "I will encourage my congregation to sing global mission hymns by ...." Bring the cards forward and place them on the worship center during the playing of "In Mission Together" on the CD.

Prayer of Dedication and Commitment

Closing Hymn: "O Zion, Haste" (#66)

J oyce D. Sohl served as Deputy General Secretary, Women's Division, The United Methodist Church from 1991 until she retired in 2004. She served as the treasurer of the Women's Division from 1976-1990. She has taught in Regional and Conference Schools of Christian Mission for over thirty years. She is a teacher, speaker, lecturer, retreat leader, writer, and musician. She wrote a monthly column in *Response* magazine for thirteen years and is the author of *Managing Our Money: A Workbook for Women and Personal Finance, A Journey in Song: Lenten Reflections on Hymns by Women,* and *Sing the Wondrous Love of Jesus: Women Hymn Writers and their Songs.* Joyce is currently serving as lay leader in her local church in White Plains, New York. She is a member of the Global Praise Working Group of the General Board of Global Ministries, a director of UMR Communications, Dallas, Texas, and a member of the Board of Overseers of Boston University School of Theology.